MW00851894

Springer Wien New York

Milena Stavrić

Predrag Šiđanin

Bojan Tepavčević

Architectural Scale Models in the Digital Age
design, representation and manufacturing

Springer Wien New York

Authors:

Dr. Milena Stavrić, Graz University of Technology, Austria
Dr. Predrag Šiđanin, University of Novi Sad, Serbia
Dr. Bojan Tepavčević, University of Novi Sad, Serbia

This book is supported as a part of a project founded by the Austrian Science Fund (FWF):
T 440 and Serbian Ministry of Education, Science and Technological Development: TR36042.

This work is subject to copyright.
All rights are reserved, whether the whole or part of the material is concerned, specifically
those of translation, reprinting, re–use of illustrations, broadcasting, reproduction by pho-
tocopying machines or similar means, and storage in data banks.

Product liability: The publisher can give no guarantee for the information contained in this
book. The use of registered names, trademarks, etc. in this publication does not imply,
even in the absence of a specific statement, that such names are exempt from the relevant
protective laws and regulations and are therefore free for general use.

© 2013 Springer–Verlag/Wien
Printed in Austria
Springer Wien New York is a part of Springer Science+Business Media
springer.at

Layout and Cover Design: Milena Stavrić, A–Graz
Proof reading: Pedro M. Lopez, A–Vienna
Printing and binding: Holzhausen Druck GmbH, A–Vienna

Printed on acid–free and chlorine–free bleached paper

SPIN: 80112724

Library of Congress Control Number: 2012953559

With 203 coloured figures

ISBN 978–3–7091–1447–6 Springer Wien New York

PREFACE

PREFACE

In the age of advanced digital technology and parametric architectural design, making physical models characterised by complex geometric forms and structural connections is a real challenge that requires adopting new approaches and applying new techniques. Physical models can be used to test and verify complex geometric forms generated with the help of virtual media, as well as to monitor their practical application. The complexity of modern architectural design requires mastering new modelling techniques, which opens a new dimension in the field of scale modelling, which is what Architectural Scale Models in the Digital Age is about. It is aimed at anyone eager to learn the basic and advanced scale modelling techniques based on examples from the field of scale modelling in contemporary architectural design.

This book is intended to fill a gap in the field of contemporary scale modelling. It focuses on connecting the main geometric principles and underlying processes of the generation of architectural forms used today with the fabrication of architectural scale models. It is divided into seven chapters, and in terms of the main topics covered, it gives a brief history of the development of the art of scale modelling, lists some possible uses of scale models in architecture and related disciplines, and presents various digital–technology–based techniques used to build physical models.

The Introduction presents the basic terms and notions used throughout the book and defines the role of the scale model in the process of architectural design development in the digital age. A brief historical overview given in Chapter 2 shows that not only have scale models always had a crucial role in construction, but their use and purpose have also reflected the cultural and historical circumstances in which they originated. Providing a short historical background is, therefore, highly relevant, as it indicates the emergence of the new, changed circumstances affecting scale modelling in the age of digital technologies.

Chapter 3 identifies a wide range of the uses of scale models in architecture and related disciplines, explaining the goals, purposes and reasons for their building today. Scale models are classified according to a number of criteria, ranging from purpose to structural form, with various cases presented to illustrate the current circumstances in which new fabrication techniques play a key role in their realisation. In connection with this, the introduction of new tools has had a major impact on the technology of physical model building.

Making scale models today requires much more than mere manual skills because the geometric structures built now are far more complex than those built before the introduction of digital technology. However, this has not ruled out the traditional ways of using manual tools, which is why an overview of both digital and traditional modelling kits and materials is given in Chapter 4.

Chapter 5 discusses the methods and processes of manufacturing scale models and scale model components, along with how they are displayed, transported, lit and photographed. It focuses on the geometric analysis of the model structure, more specifically, on the discretisation of complex forms for the purpose of preparing parts for fabrication. Basic instructions are given on how to master the principal cutting and assembly techniques.

As a follow–up, Chapter 6 contains an overview of software tools and digital fabrication techniques. It presents an array of the software most frequently used in architectural scale modelling for generating complex geometry designs. It also briefly introduces different CNC machines and rapid prototyping techniques used for model realisation.

The final chapter of the book, Chapter 7, contains five tutorials illustrating different ways in which digital technologies can be used for investigating the form in architectural design, up to the fabrication stage. Each of the tutorials begins with the theoretical explanation needed to understand the fundamental geometric principles underlying the applied procedure of generating and manufacturing the scale model.

Each chapter of Architectural Scale Models in the Digital Age ends with a reference list which may be used to further explore the discussed topics.

What the readers have before them is the result of the authors' long practical experience of studying, designing and building scale models. Original visual materials have been included to illustrate each chapter. Many of the models presented were also built and photographed exclusively for the needs of this book.

The writing and publication of this book was made possible through two projects funded by the Austrian Science Fund (FWF, Project no. T 440) and the Serbian Ministry of Education, Science and Technological Development (Project no. TR36042). We would like to hereby acknowledge our debt to all those whose advice and support were indispensible during the writing of the book. Much of the visual material contained herein was made by students from the Graz University of Technology (TU Graz), School of architecture and University of Novi Sad, Faculty of Technical Sciences (FTN), Department of Architecture and Urban Planning, and by our colleagues and friends. We owe a huge debt of gratitude to fellow academics Dejan Mitov, Albert Wiltsche, Christian Freisling, Urs Hirschberg, Ivan Marjanović, Vesna Stojaković, Marina Djurovka, Aleksandar Veselinović, Tamara Pavlović, who helped with collecting and producing the photographs. We are also thankful to Svetlana Mitić and Aleksandra Zelembabić for translating the manuscript, and to Pedro López for copy editing it. Lastly, we wish to thank our families for their support and understanding as we strove to make this book see the light of day.

CONTENTS

1 INTRODUCTION

1 INTRODUCTION

Scale modelling is a discipline that covers the construction of physical models of objects, maintaining a particular scale or relative proportions. Scale models are built for many reasons. They are made by professionals, passionate collectors and amateurs who build them as a hobby. From the professional point of view, scale models are used for different purposes. Engineers use scale models to test the performance of a particular object prototype; in the film and theatre industry they are used for scenography, whereas architects use them to prove and evaluate their ideas in different stages of project development. This book is dedicated to scale modelling as a specific field of architecture.

In the age of advanced digital techniques and parametric architectural design, making physical models of complex geometric forms and their complex structural connections is a real challenge that requires a completely new strategy, technology and technique in scale modelling. Only by using physical models can we test and verify complex geometric forms generated with virtual media, as well as control their use value. The complexity of modern architectural design requires mastering new techniques of modelling, which opens a new dimension in the field of scale modelling, which is what we address in this volume.

The word model is derived from the Latin modus and modulus, which essentially means measure [1]. The Latin terms modus and modulus have influenced the development of the wider meaning of the word model in different contexts, such as pattern or form. The architectural connotation of the term modulus was first used by a Roman architect, Marcus Vitruvius Pollio, in his treatise The Ten Books on Architecture. The Italian word modello was frequently used in the Renaissance period and it referred to the making of rough studies and detailed construction architectural models. It was later accepted in other European languages as well.

Different terms relating to scale modelling are found in different languages. The French word for model is maquette, whose original meaning was: small, preliminary model whose primary role is to visualise an idea in the architectural and artistic form [2]. The word maquette emerged in French in the late nineteenth century, and is derived from the Italian word macchietta, which means a sketch.

Scale modelling is an integral part of a broader process of architectural design and requires the ability to comprehend the relation between a designed object (the project) and its materialisation in a particular scale and material (the scale model). Methods and techniques of scale modelling enable us to assess, correct and implement a project from its earliest stages (the initial study of the form) to the conceptualisation and materialisation of the project (the main project). Different phases of design can all be identified through different approaches to building scale models, because they provide a view of each of those phases and offer a three–dimensional and spatial preview. Scale modelling strategies have a broad range of practical applications in architecture and urbanism. The building of scale models requires different techniques and procedures, as well as materials and tools. The primary advantage of using scale models is the ability to preview and identify a tangible form in material space. The material representation of the form enables the architect/designer to interact with it directly. The advantage of a scale model compared to, for example, a computer–generated drawing, or model, is that it is built in the course of the development of a project, it is part of the material construction during a dynamic working process. This process brings all segments of the project into perspective and they may be used to forecast the functioning and behaviour of the structure presented by the scale model or, if necessary, for corrections and improvements. The advantage of a material scale model compared to a computer–generated model is best seen in its tangibility – unobstructed simultaneous viewing by multiple observers from different angles. Since scale models are made of particular material and they have dimensionality that is perceived directly, no additional equipment is needed (a computer) and we can say that a scale model itself is tactile. This does not mean that digital modelling does not have any advantages compared to scale modelling, nor that its importance should be underestimated.

Computer modelling and scale modelling are in fact interrelated disciplines that use different strategies, techniques and methods to achieve the same goal – the original and quality presentation of an architectural and urbanistic work to a prospective client/audience. In fact, these two disciplines are becoming even more interrelated with the development of digital technologies and related disciplines, so that, eventually, they will become fully integrated. Computer models will be used to accurately define the materialisation of all the elements of a scale model, which is explained in this book. Scale modelling is not only learned from relevant literature, it is here to point out and help avoiding beginner's mistakes, and to choose the right technique or material. Scale modelling is a skill that is mastered through practical work and studying many available implemented examples that successfully represent preceding or derived objects. Before we continue with a more detailed explanation of the basic principles of modern scale modelling, the next chapter gives a short overview of this discipline through its historical development. It also discusses the influence of digital media on the further development of scale modelling in contemporary architectural design.

References:

[1] Gomez, A.P., Pelletier, L.: Architectural Representation and Perspective Hinge. MIT Press, Cambridge (2000)

[2] Dictionary and Thesaurus – Merriam–Webster Online (2012) Definition of Maquette. http://www.merriam–webster.com/dictionary/maquette. Accessed 12 October 2012

2 SCALE MODELLING IN ARCHITECTURE

2 SCALE MODELLING IN ARCHITECTURE

From their beginnings to the present day, scale models have reflected the cultural and historical contexts in which they were made. Scale models from different time periods can be very similar with regard to construction techniques and used materials, but the development of scale modelling as an architectural representation technique requires the consideration of their specific purpose, type and the temporal context in which they were made. Despite the development of digital techniques, construction of analogue models has not been curbed. On the contrary, digital techniques have led to even greater development and use of analogue models.

In this chapter a brief historical overview of architectural scale modelling is given in order to show to what extent temporal context and the use of existing technology reshape the process of scale modelling and architectural design. Furthermore it is shown that digital technology have shifted and changed process of design representation and thinking through scale models.

2.1   A Brief Overview

The first scale models are believed to be as old as the first drawings and, just like drawings, they have symbolised the relation between the human imagination and its symbolic representation. The purpose and use of the first scale models was different compared to their modern day application. The role of scale models as a method of testing the architectural design ideas in the modern sense is just a little more than half a millennium old.

The oldest surviving examples of scale models from ancient Egypt have been found in ancient tombs and pyramids, dating from the second millennium BC. The most significant of dozens of models found in Egyptian tombs is the one from the tomb of Mehenkwetre [4],[11] the construction foreman at the mortuary temple of Mentuhotep, dating back to the twentieth century BC. The scale models found in Egyptian tombs were built out of religious belief in the afterlife. Complete sets of figures were made to serve the ruler in the afterlife. The Egyptian models depict everyday life and people's ideas about heaven. Scale models of architectural objects were usually made sectioned or without a roof, so that their interior could be seen. Models were skilfully carved in wood or moulded in clay with a large number of details, such as door frames, window frames and stairs. The structures themselves, as well as figures inside, were painted in vibrant colours. Preserved models from ancient Egyptian tombs were not only built because the architects wanted to render the desired shape of the building for themselves and the ruler[1], but because they also had great spiritual value for their "clients" – they were a door to the serene and everlasting life after death. The cult of death and the religious system enabled the preservation of these ancient models that go back several millennia.

Greek civilization was based on a different cultural and religious system, which affected the architectural profession, the position of architects in society, and their way of thinking, designing and building. The cult of death existed in ancient Greece too, but did not have so many dramatic consequences on Greek culture, philosophy, religion and architecture. Architects did not have as high a position in society as they had in ancient Egypt, and building regulations were strictly defined, especially for public buildings and temples. Proportional relationships between the architectural elements of temples were defined by the building style. Architectural scale models did not have as much significance as the preserved specimens from the Egyptian tombs, which is why very few have been preserved. The preserved scale models were crudely made, without too much attention paid to the scale and detail, but with enough information about the character and type of the object. They were made of clay or limestone, with visible

[1] It is assumed that the architects made scale models of different objects in order to present their ideas to the Pharaon, but there is still no physical evidence.

traces of colour. The ancient Greeks had a special name for scale model: paradeigma, hence the word paradigm with a similar meaning. The Greek paradeigma did not represent a faithfully scaled replica of the original, but more a pattern, a model used to physically present the information about an architectural idea. In a similar context, paradeigma represented a model for the study of a specific architectural element, such as a triglyph or a capital [6],[8].

The influence that Greek civilisation had had on Etruscan culture and later Roman civilization was due to its colonial expansion across Southern Italy and Sicily until the seventh century BC. The Etruscan temples that were built of wood have not survived, except the foundations, but the important insight into the influence of the Greek temples on Etruscan construction is evident in the ceramic scale model of an Etruscan temple found in a tomb at Vulci. The model itself was not accurately made, but it reveals the basic features of an Etruscan temple.

Roman architecture largely relied on the Greek and Etruscan heritage while creating an architectural language based on new, alternative aesthetic principles and building technologies. The meaning and use of scale models was reinterpreted and adapted to allow for new engineering achievements. We know that the job of an architect in Roman times did not only imply designing and building houses, but also the construction of various devices, such as hydraulic pumps or siege catapults, as well as the designing of canals, dams, bridges, and seaports.

A book by the Roman architect Marcus Vitruvius Pollio, De Architectura, bears witness to the new significance that scale models had for the architects of that time. In the last chapter, describing the making and use of various devices (Latin: machine), Vitruvius writes about scale models as a tool for the testing of engineering concepts, but also as one of the methods used to convince the public of the validity and correctness of an idea – object [18]. The engineering spirit that the Roman architects had influenced the birth of a new vision for the use of scale models. At the same time, the Roman architects were aware of the downsides of scale models: the capacity and mechanical properties of materials were not always directly proportional between the scale models and the planned building.

After the division of the Roman Empire, the influence of Christianity began to spread over Eastern and Western Europe. The church had a very strong influence in the Middle Ages, which had a particular impact on architecture. Churches were "houses of God", architects were "God's builders" and scale models of churches had symbolic connotations. Therefore medieval frescoes often portrayed the rulers or founders together with a scale model of the church they were building. The church itself was a symbolic representation – a model of God's house, while the ruler/founder holding a scale model was a representation of the secular rule of the people.

Until the end of the Middle Ages, scale models remained the primary means of expression for architects. Architectural drawings were rarely made in this period, nor were they often made in previous periods[2]. According to certain medieval sources, foundations of large buildings and cathedrals were drawn in actual size on the site, while details such as windows or rosettes were carved or engraved in actual size on the walls of the building [1]. Architects tested their ideas with scale models, which remained a common practice during the Renaissance period.

Although linear, the geometric perspective is one of the most important inventions from the Renaissance period, which had a major impact on the visual arts and the shaping of the European culture in general, but scale models remain the dominant form for the representation of space in architecture.

The Renaissance architects showed great interest in scale models, discovering new goals that could be achieved by using them. It was in the Renaissance period that scale models were first given the modern meaning they have today. In the first theoretical treatise on architecture from the Renaissance period, De Re Aedificatoria (1452), Leon Battista Alberti discusses the use and significance of scale models. In this book, Alberti explains that the use of scale models permits the study of the relationship between a building and its surroundings, different parts of the structure, shape

---

[2] *A very small number of medieval drawings made by architects have been preserved until today. The surviving architectural drawings usually show a portion of a façade or architectural details.*

and size of individual architectural elements. Alberti further notes that scale models can be used to predict the cost, as the required data on the dimensions can be calculated from their elements. Most importantly, scale models can be used not only for the presentation of a building design to patrons and donors, but also as a method of developing an architectural idea. Alberti finally concludes that it is not necessary to make a detailed and realistic scale model to showcase the skill of its maker, but rather it should show the essence of the very architectural idea [2]. The significance of scale models as a method of architectural representation was also noted by other architects of the Renaissance period.

An Italian architect, painter and sculptor Filippo Brunelleschi is considered to be the first man who properly constructed the linear perspective, but also used scale models as a method for architectural presentation. During the construction of the dome of the Church of Santa Maria del Fiore, in the first half of the fifteenth century, Brunelleschi used scale models extensively. Some models were used to test the structural properties and the geometrical idea itself, while others were intended for workers and served as an explanation of how to construct specific details [14].

The importance of scale models for architects did not lessen during the sixteenth century. Instead of perspective drawings, Michelangelo Buonarroti used small clay models to test his architectural ideas. Clay models that he made for the stairs of the Laurentian Library and Saint Peter's Basilica were designed for workers to serve as a model according to which they were to build [10]. Unlike previous periods, a large number of scale models from the Renaissance period has been preserved until today. Scale models were made of different materials, usually wood, but wax was also used in the old Roman tradition of making decorative details [15].

In the Baroque period scale models were still used for presentation and the testing of architectural ideas, but drawings became an equally used method of architectural presentation. The goldsmith Hans Lencker, the author of Perspectiva Literaria (1567), was one of the first who noticed the benefits of the perspective presentation of space against scale models [12]. Lencker noted that architects had found it easier and quicker to draw perspective drawings than to build scale models out of wood or wax. However,

Baroque architects were aware of the advantages that scale models still have, compared to perspective drawings. A great Baroque sculptor and architect, Gian Lorenzo Bernini, gave more importance to the direct visual experience of scale models. Before making the final sculpture, Bernini would make three–dimensional test models out of wax or clay (Italian: bozzetti). He applied this approach when making sculptures for the fountain at the Piazza Navona, but the use of scale models served Bernini as a solution for one of the most famous squares in the world: Saint Peter's Square in Rome. According to George C. Bauer, Bernini had allegedly made seven scale models of the colonnades at St. Peter's Square in actual size, before he decided on the final shape of the ellipse [3].

The rapid development and systematisation of the techniques and conventions of architectural and engineering drawing began after the baroque period, culminating in the birth of descriptive geometry, a new discipline in applied mathematics. Despite the development of drawing techniques, the interest in scale modelling remained almost unchanged and without significant innovation up until the period of contemporary architecture. A new way of using scale models emerged at the turn of the twentieth century, in the work of a Catalan architect, Antoni Gaudi. Gaudi's architecture is unique in many aspects and largely originated from his views on religion, symbolism and the aesthetics of the geometric form.

He was very religious and he spent 40 years working on the project of the Church of Sagrada Familia (Fig. 2.1). Like the builders of Gothic cathedrals, Gaudi used the symbolism of geometry to describe divine perfection. Unlike his predecessors and contemporaries, he thought of ruled surfaces and especially hyperbolic paraboloids as symbols of perfection, which he compared with the holy trinity [5]. Knowing that this type of geometry is impossible or very difficult to define on paper, he encouraged the search for a new approach to the research and creation of the architectural forms. In some of his projects, such as the crypt of the Church of Colònia Güell, Gaudi used wire models, which self–generated their form under the influence of gravity and their load (Fig. 2.2).

Fig. 2.1 *A model of Sagrada Familia at Minimundus, Klagenfurt. Architect: Antoni Gaudi*

He made different complex geometric shapes in this way, depending on the length of chains or ropes and the hanging position. At the same time, the wire system was a solution for defining static systems in which only axial forces occur.

Gaudi later used the "mirror image" of a model that served him as a basis for sketching the building [16]. Gaudi's approach to the study of form has had a double significance. Scale models were first used as a method of self–generation of form. On the other hand, the created form, although geometrically complex, had a statically stable configuration with axial forces only.

At the beginning of the twentieth century modern scale models were extensively used as a way of testing new architectural ideas or researching the sensitivity of materials. The avant–garde trends in arts and architecture during the first half of the twentieth century were influenced by new concepts of space reflecting the idea of the relativity of space and time. New scientific discoveries, such as the theory of relativity and the concept of four–dimensional space–time, soon grew into broad cultural and social phenomena. Various new art movements emerged, such as cubism and futurism, which portrayed form in motion that could

Fig. 2.2 *A model of Sagrada Familia by Gaudi. A wire model that can self–generate the form under the influence of gravity and the load. A mirror image (the mirror is on the floor) gives a true image of the final form*

be seen from more than one viewing point simultaneously. Similarly, architectural objects were designed so that their composition could be seen by moving around the object, rather than from a predefined or preferred perspective.

This approach involved the viewing of an object from the bird's eye perspective, which is why the "fifth façade", or roof plane, became such an important part of spatial composition. Although they could be used to present an entire project, drawings did not suffice for this new way of seeing architecture, formed by the architects of Modernism. Instead, just like sculpture, architectural scale modelling became an art form whose composition and volumetric relations could be tested by viewing them from all sides. Such an analogy between sculpture and architectural model is most prominent in the conceptual research of the project Architectonics by Kazimir Malevich, as well as in the project for the Monument to the Third International, by the Russian constructivist Vladimir Tatlin. Other followers of the architectural avant–garde in the first half of the twentieth century, such as Theo van Doesburg, Cornelis van Eesteren, Le Corbusier and Frank Lloyd Wright, also used scale models. For Wright, by his own admission, it was the experience of playing with wooden froebl cubes in his early childhood that had influenced him. Geometric forms that he produced by stacking and combining these cubes, had a strong influence on Wright's attitude towards architectural form [19].

Modernist architects used scale models to study the compositional ratio of volume to the shadow it casts, viewing it from different angles. A particularly interesting attitude towards scale models was discovered in a project by Ludwig Mies van der Rohe, in the competition for the business building/skyscraper at Friedrichstrasse in Berlin. Scale models were made of glass, photographed and then inserted in the photomontage. In the description that accompanied his first proposal for this competition, Mies wrote: "My efforts with an actual glass model helped me to recognize that the most important thing about using glass is not the effects of light and shadow, but the rich play of reflection" [17]. The foundations of the building had an irregular, seemingly arbitrary shape, but the glass membrane of the scale model revealed the basic concept of the building: the ratio of reflection between the surrounding buildings to the transparency of the façade, depending on the angle and the position of viewing.

In the middle of the twentieth century, a number of architects were interested in complex geometric forms. The Berlin Philharmonic Hall by architect Hans Scharoun, Sydney Opera House by Jørn Utzon, TWA Terminal at the New York International Airport by Eero Saarinen and the chapel in Ronchamp by Le Corbusier are all examples of buildings with complex curved, non–orthogonal geometric forms, built in the nineteen–fifties. In the mentioned examples, the research process progressed from initial sketches through to scale models to technical drawings. One of the first architects who introduced the exploration of free form with scale models was Frederick Kiesler. Kiesler's 1959 Endless House project anticipated the appearance of Blob architecture that emerged in the late twentieth century. He made scale models out of clay or plaster–coated mesh netting. Kiesler's approach was at the same time both architectural and sculptural, while the complex forms that he made with scale models were impossible to build until the beginning of the twentieth century, when digital technologies were developed. The complex form of the chapel at Ronchamp required different types of scale models in relation to their purpose, as well as accurate coordination between the main architect and the associates who were interpreting his ideas. Le Corbusier was using the initial sketches, which his associate, Joseph Savina, would then convert into plaster models, with a little help from his imagination. After the construction of the working models, an additional model would be made of wire, with a paper coating that served as an aid in solving the engineering drawings and structural elements [7].

During the construction of the most famous building on the Australian continent – Sydney Opera House – Jørn Utzon used scale models as a means of testing his architectural concepts (Fig. 2.3). After winning the competition for the Sydney Opera House in 1957, Jørn Utzon, together with his team of engineers and architects, spent four years trying to find an adequate solution for the complex geometrical assignment demanded by the shape of the building. After having explored different forms, from ellipsoids to paraboloids, Jørn Utzon found an elegant solution in 1961, using sphere segments as models for the roof structure.

According to his own words, he found the inspiration for this concept while cutting an orange into slices, and he tested the idea with a conceptual wooden scale model – sphere

– from which segments of different sizes were carefully cut out as elements of the roof structure (Fig. 2.4).

Fig. 2.3 *The exhibition model of the Sydney Opera House*

The use of sphere segments was also an ingenious structural solution at the same time. The degree of curvature is the same throughout, therefore the construction of roof shells demanded the use of only one movable form. This is why Utzon used a conceptual scale model in his project to satisfy both the compositional and structural demands.

During the second half of the twentieth century, a number of buildings emerged representing new advances in structural engineering. Pier Luigi Nervi became famous in the sixties with his ribbed concrete structures, prefabricated halls and stadiums. He found the inspiration for his structures in the organic forms whose supporting structures follow the lines of forces. In the description for the ribbed ceiling of the Gatti Wool Factory, Nervi says: "The arrangement of the ribs correspond to the isostatics of the main point in a system subject to stress" [13]. Felix Candela, a Spanish engineer, is another one of the major constructors of this period, who tried to demonstrate the great potential of curved concrete shells by using hyperbolic paraboloids (Fig. 2.5).

Fig. 2.4 *Jørn Utzon's idea for the construction of the roof shells of Sydney Opera House. Bronze plate – model, displayed in front of the Sydney Opera House, a replica of the original scale model of the sphere with wooden slices*

This potential relates to the elegance of the form, minimal use of materials and the exceptional combination of fundamental surfaces aimed at obtaining new aesthetic values of the architectural forms.

Fig. 2.5 Scale model of curved concrete shells by using hyperbolic paraboloids – Felix Candela

In the 1970s, a German engineer and architect, Frei Otto, became interested in the process of self–generating forms (Fig. 2.6) and membrane structures, leading to renewed interest in the scale modelling method used by Antoni Gaudi. Apart from his architectural education, Frei Otto had also been trained in structural engineering, which made It possible to explore form in a unique way, since he considered physical models to be solutions to the mathematical and structural problems of minimal surfaces. This approach enabled him to create completely new and unexpected spatial solutions, such as the Olympic Stadium in Munich or Mannheim Multihalle in Mannheim.

Fig. 2.6 The study of form through the use of scale models of self–generating surfaces. The scale model that was built after Frei Otto's model. The model is made of paper clips that are grouped into hexagonal segments

During the 1990s, a Spaniard, Santiago Calatrava continued the tradition of Nervi, Candela, Isler (Fig. 2.7) and others. He found the inspiration for his projects in nature and the constructive systems of living organisms (Fig. 2.8). Having degrees in both architecture and structural engineering gives

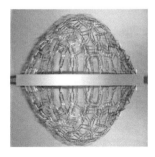

his structures a recognisable identity, with an emphasis on elegance and exquisite balance between mass and force. He is also a painter and a sculptor. The basic geometric principles of his famous buildings can be seen in sculptural models, which are the first stage in the design process.

Fig. 2.7 Study model of "Hanging cloth" Heinz Isler

Fig. 2.8 The Opera House and Cultural Centre of the Palau de les Arts, Valencia. Architect Santiago Calatrava

Apart from the initial sketch, a scale model is also the inspiration and starting point for Frank Gehry in his designs. His working models are made of sheets of paper and folded to the point of maximum curvature. Given that these structures do not follow any natural laws, the transfer of a working model into the design model is done by scale model scanning (reverse engineering). Therefore, his structures are recognisable by their free form (Fig. 2.9) which, in its

geometrical structure, derives from the developmental sur-
faces (Fig. 2.10). The most recent projects by Shigeru Ban,
Centre Pompidou–Metz (2010) and Haesley Nine Bridges
Golf Club House in South Korea (2011), have merged Frei
Otto's membranes and Pier Luigi Nervi's ribbed structures.

Fig. 2.9 *Walt Disney – Con-
cert Hall, Frank O. Gehry &
Partners*

Fig. 2.10 *The scale model
of the Novartis building by
Frank O. Gehry & Partners
– part of the Masterplan for
Novartis in Basel, arch. Vitto-
rio Magnano Lampugnani*

The inspiration for the constructive solution of these free
forms came from a hexagonal mesh netting model (Fig.
2.11), found in the weave of Chinese knitted hats.

Today, we are aware of the fact that in terms of shape, architectural objects have become sculptural forms that seem
to know no limits in the selection of form, material and con-

struction systems. These changes have largely resulted from the introduction of computer software in the field of design. One thing is sure: scale models in this age have achieved new significance and developed further largely due to the onset of digital techniques.

Fig. 2.11 *The scale model of the Centre Pompidou in Metz – a hexagonal mesh roof supporting structure, arch. Shigeru Ban*

2.2 The Influence of digital media on the development of scale modelling

In the 1980s, with the development of technology and the use of Computer Aided Design (CAD) software in architectural design, the position of scale models and drawings has significantly changed. Drawings made with rapidograph pens have been replaced with drawings made in CAD, while scale models – analogue models – have been replaced with digital models in virtual 3D environments.

In the conceptual phase of design, digital models in a virtual environment are much easier to make than analogue models. The possibilities for modifications are endless. Thus the digital models are a much cheaper and faster means of representing space. However, practice has shown that these virtual models have often been idealised, introduced and presented in a way that differs from the virtual model in real, human three–dimensional space. So after the initial euphoria of presenting objects in the 3D world, the presentation of structures with scale models has been given even greater significance. In fact, in architectural contests around the world, it is compulsory to submit a scale model in the appropriate scale, together with two–dimensional drawings. These contests usually have a "master model" into which every competitor's work is "inserted." This is how the quality of a project is analysed and the work rated.

At this moment, the power of digital technology is undeniable, with the possibility to make presentations through rendering (realistic images) and different types of animation (films), but experience has already confirmed that scale models remain one of the most convincing ways of presenting architectural projects.

In the 1990s, virtual modelling continued to develop with the introduction of Building Information Modelling (BIM). BIM is an information model in which, apart from the geometric characteristics, the designed object can be given qualitative and quantitative information, as well as data on the spatial disposition of the individual structural parts and their lifecycle. A growing number of architecture software packages today has the ability to support BIM technology. Since BIM technology is based on data safekeeping, visualization and the transformation of data into information, it is a very current topic in the field of architecture. A combination of analogue 3D scale models [9] and digital dynamic mapping methods (enrichment of 3D modelling) for the required information is used for this purpose (Fig. 2.12 and Fig. 2.13).

Fig. 2.12 *An analogue model of Styria and a dynamic information system, a project implemented as part of the 2010 study: "Zersiedelung Steiermark" at the Institute of Architecture and Media, Graz*

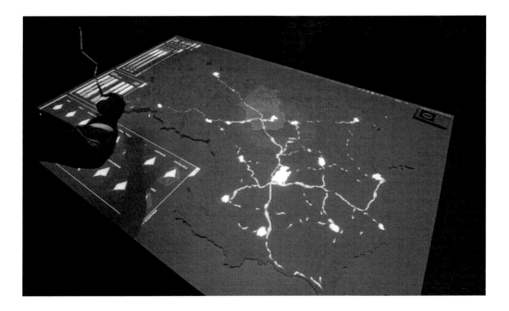

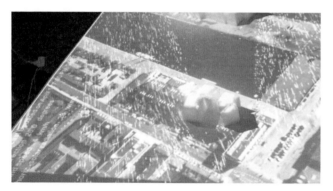

Fig. 2.13 *Smart Geometry Workshop 2011,"Interacting with the city", dynamic mapping of information about the wind in Copenhagen*

Digital techniques have contributed much more to scale modelling than the presentation of three–dimensional objects in a virtual environment. This primarily relates to development in geometric terms. With the use of NURBS technology in architectural design at the beginning of the twentieth century, architectural projects became more and more complicated in geometric terms. Digital media have enabled a different working methodology for scale modelling with the appropriate fabrication methods, primarily concerning the rate of construction, which is further explained in Chapter 6. In any case, one thing is undeniable: the future of scale modelling is in the synthesis of analogue methods and digital technology, which opens up an interesting and creative environment for the development of scale modelling.

2.3   The importance of scale models for contemporary design

Contemporary architectural design surprises us every day by setting new standards in the selection of forms and structural solutions for architectural projects. Thus the importance of scale models in contemporary design has a new dimension.

Digital possibilities in the field of NURBS modelling have revolutionised the field of design in architecture. One of the changes relates to the development of free–form structures, which is why there is a growing number of such projects and constructed buildings in contemporary practice. These buildings have very complex geometry, as compared to standard architectural projects, and require specialised construction techniques. With these objects, standard connection elements and materials cannot be used and a unique solution has to be found for each object. From this point of view, each of these projects is unique (Fig. 2.14).

Given the high complexity of these structures, which are called non–standard architecture in practice, the position of scale models in contemporary design has gained a qualitative significance. Namely, the measurability of structure complexities in a design phase can only be seen if such a non–standard structure is broken down into individual parts and a prototype model is made in the appropriate scale.

Fig. 2.14 *Non–standard structure, Water Flux, arch. R&Sie(n), exhibition "Re–sampling Ornament", 2009, Museum of Architecture in Stockholm*

These parts are usually different so that their assembly requires thorough structural analysis of the individual parts, their labelling and logistics in the assembling. Since it comes to forms of objects that deviate from traditional structures, compared to known static conditions, the entire structure is controlled by means of scale models with different static impacts. This book puts a special emphasis on the importance of scale models in the digital era, their use, role and construction methods.

References:

[1] Ackerman, J.S.: Origins, Imitation, Conventions: Representation in the Visual Arts. MIT Press, Cambridge (2002)

[2] Alberti, L.B.: On the Art of Building in ten Books, De Re Aedificatoria (trans: Rykwert, J., Tavernor, R., Leach, N.). MIT Press, Cambridge (1988)

[3] Bauer, G.C.: From architecture to scenography: The full–scale model in the baroque tradition. In: Schnapper, A.(ed.) La Scenografia barocca, pp. 141–149. Clueb, Bologna (1979)

[4] Bourriau, J.: Pharaohs and Mortals: Egyptian Art in the Middle Kingdom. Cambridge University Press, Cambridge (1988)

[5] Collins, G.R.: Antonio Gaudi (Masters of World Architecture). George Braziller, New York (1960)

[6] Coulton, J.J.: Ancient Greek Architects at Work: Problems of Structure and Design. Cornell University Press, Ithaca (1977)

[7] Evans, R.: The Projective Cast: Architecture and its Three Geometries. MIT Press, Cambridge (2000)

[8] Hahn, R.: Anaximander and the Architects – The Contributions of Egyptian and Greek Architectural Technologies to the Origins of the Greek Philosophy. SUNY Press, New York (2001)

[9] Institute for Architecture and media: https://iam2.tugraz.at/studio/s10/, Accessed 14 Jun 2012

[10] Kostof, S.: The Architect: Chapters in the History of the Profession. Oxford University Press, New York (1977)

[11] Mackenzie, D.A.: Daily life in ancient Egypt – Mehenkwetre Tomb. AAA Encyclopedia. http://www.kenseamedia.com/encyclopedia/ddd/daily_life1.htm (2012). Accessed 15 Sep 2012

[12] Peiffer, J.: Constructing perspective in sixteenth–century Nuremberg. In: Carpo, M., Lemerle, F. (eds.) Perspective, Projections, and Design: Technologies of Architectural Representation, pp. 65–76. Routledge, London (2007)

[13] Portoghesi, P. : Nature and Architecture. Skira, Milan (2000)

[14] Prager, F.F., Scaglia, G.: Brunelleschi: Studies of his Technology and Inventions. Dover Publications, Mineola (2004)

[15] Smith, A.C.: Architectural Model as Machine: A New View of Models from Antiquity to the Present Day. Architectural Press Elsevier, Oxford (2004)

[16] Smith, S.K.: Architects' Drawings – A Selection of Sketches by World Famous Architects Through History. Elsevier, Oxford (2005)

[17] Van der Rohe, L.M.: Hochhausprojekt für Bahnhof Friedrichstraße. Frühlicht 1. pp.122–124 (1922)

[18] Vitruvius, M.P.: De architectura. English edition: Vitruvius MP (1914) The Ten Books on Architecture (trans: Morgan MH). http://www.gutenberg.org/files/20239/20239–h/29239–h.htm (2006). Accessed 15 Feb 2011

[19] Wright, F.L.: A Testament. Horizon Press, New York (1957)

3 THE USE OF SCALE MODELS IN ARCHITECTURE

3 THE USE OF SCALE MODELS IN ARCHITECTURE

Scale models have been used throughout almost the entire history of architecture. Today, scale modelling is used in architecture for different reasons: from the exploration of the form, to the presentation or display of architectural details and correlations. Therefore, there are several possible objectives when building scale models: to explore the form, the level of detail and properties of an object, to decide on an appropriate planning strategy, and many others that go beyond the scope of architectural design. An object can be presented by a scale model in different ways and at different stages of its creation. Their purpose changes with the different spatial display tasks: from the display of internal spaces/interiors to city models. This chapter discusses the purpose of scale modelling, types of scale models in architecture and city planning, and their scales in greater length.

3.1   The purpose of scale modelling

The purpose of scale models is to present objects, their context and/or details in the most realistic way possible. How objects are presented with scale models depends on the project development stage. Every architectural design stage can include relevant scale models. Every version of the project can also have its own appropriate variation of scale models. The level of scale model detailing depends on the project stage it illustrates, or the presentation strategy for the designed objects. Logically, while still at the initial schematic design stage, scale models cannot show details that have not yet been defined. It should be kept in mind that when the main project for an object has been completed or when the object itself has already been completed (or is already in use), scale models can show even the smallest details. Hence every scale model follows a specific objective and has a specific purpose chosen by its designer, mostly to be able to examine different aspects of the project.

3.1.1   Exploration of the form

One of the first early design stages is to study the required functions and find the appropriate object form. Conceptual scale models are used to explore all the shapes that have architectural potential [2],[5]. They do not have to be related to a particular architectural project, but address a particular type of spatial problem or exploration. Conceptual scale models are rarely based on realistic design task frameworks of or specific functional requirements.

In addition to conceptual scale models, the exploration of architectural form also requires the use of working scale models. Working scale models are simple and "incomplete" models made of easily processed materials (paper, cardboard, styrofoam, etc.) and without much detailing. Usually, a number of these models are made, one for each planned version. Designers primarily use them to examine the volume, correlation between the shapes and their sizes, connection with the environment, etc. The purpose of working models is to define, redefine or correct errors in the architectural design process.

Usually a number of conceptual variants or working models are made. They are also used to document the development/generation of ideas and forms they illustrate (Fig. 3.1). Scale models are often photographed for records and to illustrate the development of ideas. Projects can be developed using digital modelling techniques parallel to the exploration of shapes with scale models.

These two methods employ completely different techniques and approaches to scale modelling, but are based on identical principles that complement each other and contribute to a more comprehensive examination of future projects. Making changes to the form and volume in CAD is very simple and allows for very rapid changes and analyses of the form. The biggest shortcoming of digital modelling is the lack of materiality (regardless of the different types of rendering techniques) and realistic three–dimensionality of objects (regardless of the virtual 3D environment), which can only be realised with the help of physical scale models.

Digital and analogue modelling techniques can thus be con-sidered complementary tools. Digital technologies have led to the development of non–standard architectural projects, whose complex geometric structure is based on the use of free–form surfaces (Fig. 3.2).

If conceptual solutions are based on the geometry of free–form surfaces, then the design process includes a series of working models to test the structural solutions, as well as the correlation between the details and the possibilities of project realisation. Fig. 3.2 gives an example of the development of a non–standard project, from the conceptual stage

Fig. 3.1 *The development of an architectural shape through the process of build-ing working scale models, up: roof study, down: final model, The Sage Gateshead, Foster + Partners, Art Muse-um Shanghai*

through to implementation. The main concept of the project lies in the double–curved surfaces planarization (1) and the analysis of the possible forms of the planarized parts (2). Further analysis is found in the CAD model definition (3), the working model definition (4), 3D print model (5), working model of the structural connections between individual elements (6), production of individual templates for connecting elements (7), details in the final connection between elements (8) and the final detail (9) of the individual element connections (elements are made of cross laminated timber of 95mm thickness) and realisation of the object (10, 11) [3].

Fig. 3.2 *Development of the project, starting from the conceptual model, through working models, CAD models and detailing model to the completed object. FWF project: "Non–Standard Architecture with Ornaments and Planar Elements", Graz University of Technology; Institute for Architecture und Media*

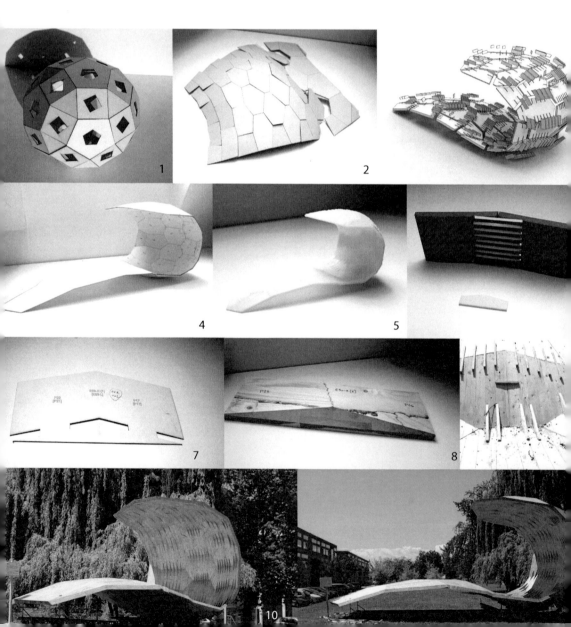

3.1.2   Presentation of constructed objects and their surroundings

Usually scale models are not made after the finalisation of function and form, nor during work on the technical development of architectural structure projects. Once the project is complete, it is then possible to build a presentation model. Presentation models are generally built with a high degree of detail (Fig. 3.3). Scale models of already constructed objects are made with different objectives.

Fig. 3.3 Detailed presentation model of the Pompidou – Metz Centre

They usually represent buildings of great public importance (city halls, libraries, convention centres, shopping malls, airports, etc.), whose appearance is in a way different from the usual shapes (or structural systems), with the aim of analysing the object as a whole. Scale models of structures built long ago are often made because of their historical significance for a specific area. Those representing architectural heritage structures are the most common parts of museum collections. Scale models are made with great attention to detail, often so that certain parts can be opened to reveal the interior of an object. Models are accurately and realistically materialised, and they often incorporate lighting effects. They can be enclosed in glass or plexiglass cases to avoid damage. Scale models are also built to represent objects whose design was significantly modified during construction, which is when the design project of the constructed object is also made to facilitate the maintenance of the object itself. In this case, scale models of constructed objects represent the constructed object design, or structures of architectural heritage merit.

Presentation models are often made to communicate specific architectural forms in the context of a wider (urban) situation [2],[5]. These specific models are called site models (Fig. 3.4). Site models represent the surroundings of designed or constructed objects. Site scale models can also be built to represent objects that are yet to be designed and are then usually made in the earliest design stages.

In public architectural competitions these models are often mounted on a display stand or a base. Their purpose is to communicate the idea of a large complex design. Site models should not be mistaken for city models, which represent wider city areas, although the scale can be the same. Master plan models are a type of city models representing city planning projects, being themselves a part of them. They are made to the same scale as projects they illustrate, thus being stripped of excessive detailing, depending on the scale. Master plan models (Fig. 3.5) represent city blocks with buildings, streets, squares, canals, railways, river banks and all those urban elements/objects incorporated into the project.

Fig. 3.4 Site model – Maritime Museum and Science Centre in Budapest

City models representing the current city situation and often its historical core, are usually displayed in halls of important city institutions, such as city halls or other public buildings. City models made in bronze are sometimes placed in famous city centre squares, open and publicly available to everyone. In time, they develop an extra layer of patina (see also Fig. 3.9).

Fig. 3.5 Model of the Downtown Area of Central Shanghai, Shanghai Urban Planning Exhibition Center

3.1.3   Presentation of details and characteristics of objects

Detail models are built for many reasons. They are most commonly built to a scale large enough to easily see the details. Interior models are architectural models often built to show interior space details, colours and materials (scale of 1:10 or 1:25). These models can be quite charming because of the freedom in the project presentation and the freedom of expression in the use of colour, structure and material. Models are useful in the selection of an object's structural systems or the analysis of other object characteristics (Fig. 3.6). This is precisely the reason for which some scale models are built: to emphasise specific characteristics of objects (Fig. 3.7).

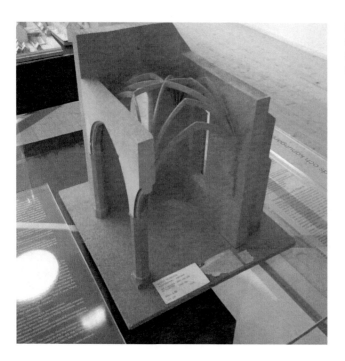

Fig. 3.6 A scale model of an arched ceiling structural detail, Museum of Architecture in Stockholm

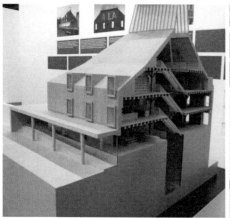

3.1.4   Selecting adequate planning strategies

Fig. 3.7 A scale model of a structural system, ETH Zürich

Scale models can also play an important role in the approval of key strategic projects, as well as in high–level political decision–making (regional, interstate, etc.) [1]. This is city or spatial planning, where viewing of a wider area can be very difficult. Apart from the presentation of objects (e.g. highways, bridges, power stations, etc.) to a specific scale, these scale models also use contour lines, becoming relief

maps that show the planned land levelling, as well as the
existing vegetation and the planned landscaping, the level
of flooding (if there is a river), etc. In this case, scale models
are used to show the most important project aspects without too much detailing (Fig. 3.8) , depending on the available budget. It is much easier to see the main advantages
or disadvantages of different strategic project variations in
scale models, than in project documentation, which by no
means minimises the importance of such documentation in
reaching a final decision, since it is in fact crucial to the examination of strategically important project quality.

Scale models can provide primary, i.e. visual information
about projects. Decision makers use scale models to form
their opinions (pre–selection), which are later confirmed
or adjusted in the course of a detailed examination of a
project's documentation. Therefore, scale models are not
conclusive, they are indicators that draw attention to a particular project. It is very important in this case (as well as in
all other cases) that scale models be built accurately and to
high quality standards.

Fig. 3.8 Tsunami affected
area, SANAA, 13th International Architecture Exhibition
– Common Graund, Venice,
2012

3.1.5   Other purposes of scale modelling

Apart from scale models used by architects and city and spatial planners in their work, there are other types of scale models used by professionals in other fields. The following paragraphs discuss several types of scale models whose purpose is not necessarily closely related to architecture. Scale models are often built to showcase the range of features (Fig. 3.9). A bronze scale model of Hamburg large building complexes offer to their audience/visitors (e.g. showgrounds, amusement parks, large tourist complexes, airports, shopping malls, national parks, etc.). Exhibitions models are made after the structure has been built, before or during the official opening.

Fig. 3.9 *A bronze scale model of Hamburg*

Most of the time they are completely realistic, with a high degree of detailing and additional information (primarily about different routes and distances). Scale models made for this purpose are usually enclosed in glass or plexiglass boxes to protect them from damage and displayed at the building complex entrance (Fig. 3.10). These models are often equipped with special lighting so that they can be clearly seen at night or in bad weather.

Scale models are often used in different art fields such as sculpture, stage design, applied arts and industrial design. These models are made to communicate ideas or their variations in cheaper materials of smaller dimensions that are easily and quickly processed (Fig. 3.11).

Fig. 3.10 Exhibition model (left) at the building complex entrance of the Westmount Square in Montréal (right), arch. Ludwig Mies van der Rohe

Fig. 3.11 A scale model in stage design – built by students at the Arts and Design Academy in Milan

Scale stage and theatre design models are built for many reasons. Their purpose is to enable all participants in a production (the director, actors, technical staff, etc.) to understand the context and entirety of the production, including scene changes (stage or production design). Scale models help actors in the initial stages of lines rehearsals to become familiar with set and scene changes during rehearsals and the performance. Scale models can also be part of the set (Fig. 3.12) .

Whether stage design or sculpture, industrial design or applied arts such as pottery, the purpose of scale models is to present the work to someone (often the artists themselves)

who will decide on the direction of its further development in a more permanent material and the appropriate applicable scale. In sculpture, models are usually made of cheap materials (e.g. plaster or wax) to analyze the volume and form of sculptures and their future position in space. Scale models are sometimes a prerequisite to compete for the construction of public monuments (sculptures).

In the film and television industry (Fig. 3.13), scale models and mock ups are used to achieve certain effects that this medium supports (explosions, demolitions, collisions, spacecrafts, etc.), and for economic reasons.

Fig. 3.12 Scale models in theatre design – a scene from the production of Images of "My World" by a theatre group from Stara Pazova

Fig. 3.13 Mock Up at the "Bavaria Filmstadt München"

Scale models in the applied arts and industrial design are mostly product prototypes and are used for different types of testing. They are often made in small batches, and each new model is modified with reference to the previous one. Scale modelling in all fields, including art, is based on the same principle as in architecture, only to different scales and for different purposes.

Scale models are also built for fun, play or as a hobby. Scale modelling in this context is often called model making. Models made this way are tailored to suit different themes, such as model planes (that can or cannot fly), model railways, model cars, miniature building complexes or miniature landscapes. Model makers make models as a hobby, for competitions or they simply collect them.

Models used as tourist attractions are made for similar reasons. In many countries there are tourist complexes featuring important architectural structures (Fig. 3.14) or objects relevant to specific regions. Similar objects are often made to a 1:25 scale. They are very realistic and made of materials resistant to atmospheric changes, as exhibition grounds are often exposed to the elements.

Fig. 3.14 *Scale model of the Dutch Parliament, miniature city Madurodam, The Hague, Netherlands*

Tourist attractions featuring models such as these are visited by tens of thousands of tourists from around the world each year, proving to be a successful concept that is used more and more.

Models are also made for cultural and educational reasons, and as museum exhibits. These models represent different objects in connection with the architectural heritage (Fig. 3.15), ethnology, or specific archaeological sites, or perhaps even futuristic visions of the future. They are always built with realistic detailing and are the best way to represent their real–life equivalents. Such models are often part of special museum displays or thematic exhibitions. Most of the time they are part of a bigger presentation of research themes, illustrating specific segments, lifestyles and cultures. Scale models illustrate historical representations of long past eras, or are futuristic visions of possible developments and lifestyles.

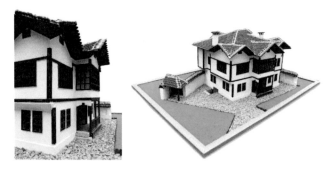

Fig. 3.15 *Scale models of the complex Konak Malog Riste, museum in Ponisavlje, Pirot*

As already discussed, scale models are made for many reasons. In addition to the mentioned purposes in the context of different professional and personal reasons, scale models are also built for educational purposes. So–called training models are built for educational purposes and they usually do not represent architectural objects.

Training models are scale models built for training needs, mainly in the field of complex technological process management (e.g. in refineries, factories, power plants, etc.) or equipment management (vessels, aircraft, locomotives, spacecraft, etc.). Training models are built to large scales (1:2 or 1:5) or life–size scale (1:1). It is much cheaper to build training models using the same materials and the same functional characteristics of the objects they represent. These models are then used to train a large number of people who will operate the actual equipment, than to let them use their limited knowledge on devices that often cost millions of Euros, risking damaging, destruction and possible casualties immediately after their theoretical training. Another difference between training models and classic educational models is that they are almost always connected with the cutting–edge technology they represent.

3.2   Types of architectural scale models

In the previous section we discussed the main reasons for building architectural and similar scale models. In this section we briefly discuss the basic types of scale models. Models can be divided into many categories and by many criteria [1],[2],[4],[5],[6]. Generally, architectural models in this book are divided following three core criteria (Fig. 3.16), namely: 1) their purpose, 2) the spatial level they represent and 3) the structural system they represent.

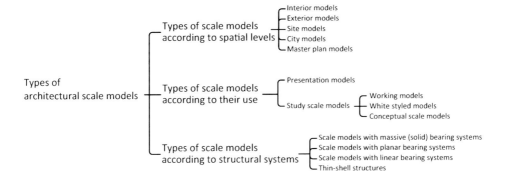

3.2.1   Types of scale models according to their use

Fig. 3.16 Division of architectural models by different aspects

In relation to purpose, scale models can be divided into two basic groups: primary – study scale models and secondary – exhibition scale models. Primary or study scale models are: conceptual, working and white, styled scale models. Study models are scale models built to analyse and study specific correlations, such as volume, height, communication, etc.

Conceptual scale models (Fig. 3.17) are built in initial project stages to explore the abstract qualities such as materiality, interpretation motifs, correlations between shapes and illumination (light and shadow), or between the solid and hollow. Conceptual models are made of different materials, not only to explore the future project concepts, but also to analyse certain physical characteristics of the material. Experiences like these also represent a starting point for the definition of the structural systems of the analysed forms. These models can be seen as specific forms of scale drawings used as "development code" to communicate the creation of architectural ideas [6]. Idea development can progress by using different means, such as making paper cuts out of scale drawings, or using and playing (experimentation) with specific geometrical shapes (e.g. with LEGO Bricks).

Fig. 3.17 *Different conceptual scale models defining concepts and techniques*

The development of ideas is an incredible creative process that encompasses overall knowledge, experiences, feelings, conditions, situations, etc. Close observation of the conceptual model development defines initial positions and different ideas for possible project development. Although their use as development information is similar, their conceptual essence is different and illustrates to what extent conceptual approach levels can vary.The beginning of work on conceptual scale models is tied to the original idea and sketches that are usually two–dimensional. More specifically, conceptual models are a means of giving the ideas sketched on paper a form in space. Fig. 3.18 shows sketches, inspirational design elements and simple tools needed for the realisation of the first sketch and conceptual models.

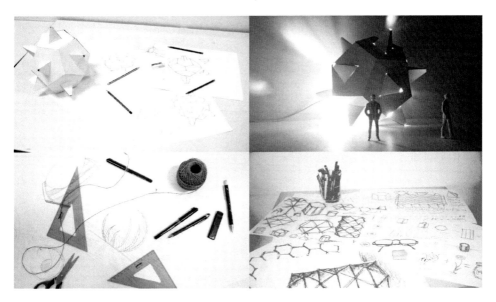

Conceptual scale models became especially important at the end of the twentieth century, when the idea of transformable structures began to develop intensively through scale models. The idea of deployable and transformable structures in architecture (folding architecture) is relatively new and offers new potential not only in the field of form exploration, but also in building and transportation possibilities. In terms of paper folding[1]

Fig. 3.18 A sketch as starting point for a conceptual scale model and the transfer of the idea from a 2D medium into the three–dimensional space

1 Paper folding and cutting techniques are also known as origami and kirigami. Origami is the ancient Japanese art of paper folding (Japanese: ori = folding, disassemble, kami = paper), and kirigami (Japanese: kiri = to cut, kami = paper) is a variation of origami that includes cutting small paper cuts, creating even more interesting solutions.

and cutting possibilities, conceptual scale models have led the way in a new field in architectural research (Fig. 3.19). Different patterns for folding and cutting paper, as well as origami patterns, have had a major influence on the development of conceptual architectural models. Paper folding offers a simple and intuitive way to explore shapes.

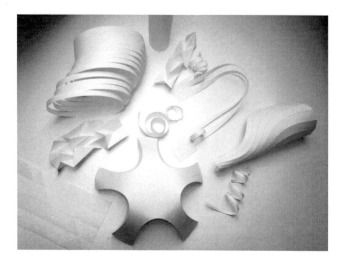

Fig. 3.19 *Paper as inspiration for conceptual scale models*

At the same time, new research in this direction has raised new questions and standards in terms of structural systems exploration. The analogy between the techniques and possibilities of paper folding has been recognised and identified in the possibilities of folding and unfolding of the board materials architectural objects can be made of. Certain origami pattern types make it possible to reduce the volume of objects by folding them down. This in turn facilitates their quick, easy transport and unfolding on–site, where they cover large spaces. At the same time, origami patterns can be used to make complex geometric forms whose shape can be simply changed by moving specific parts of models. Given that this topic is very interesting with regard to scale modelling, folding techniques are discussed in more detail in Chapter 7. This chapter covers the basic principles of folding and pattern development and also gives numerous examples that may serve as inspiration for architectural design.

The simultaneous cutting and folding of board materials offers another field of exploration for conceptual models. Using a series of perforations on a material can affect the material properties, reducing its rigidity and giving it extra flexibility. Fig. 3.20 shows two different ways of cutting the same material – paper – with very different folding transformation possibilities. If a thicker material is cut the same way, folding has a completely different effect. Density, direction and length of the cuts in this case directly affect the flexibility of the material and shaping possibilities (Fig. 3.21).

Fig. 3.20 *Different ways of cutting paper, giving it different shapes when folded*

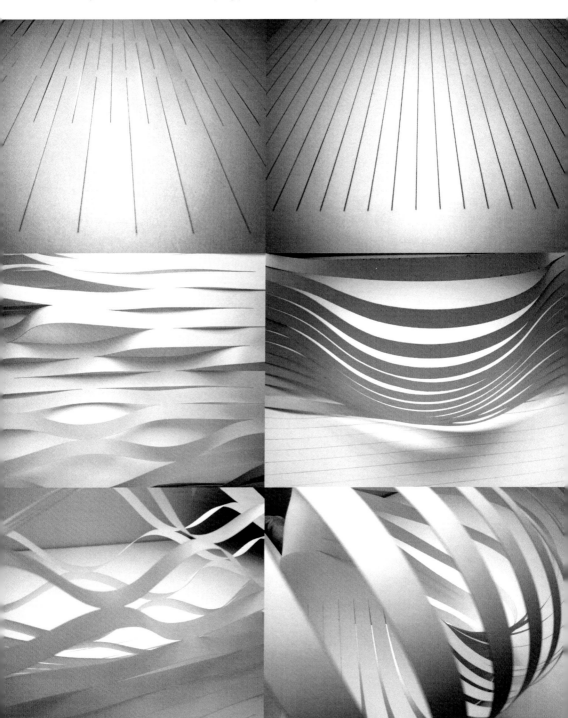

At the same time, perforations made on the material allow light to pass through. The correlation between light and shadows in perforated materials offers great potential for the study of space in architecture.

The basic significance of conceptual scale models lies in the discovery of new possibilities and potentials of the architectural space. Their use, production and development can play a key role in later design stages.

Digital techniques such as 3D modelling or laser cutting can be extremely useful in the conceptual design stages. A very intuitive use of simple 3D software, such as SketchUp, allows for fast 3D modelling and modification. CAD modelling unfortunately does not offer the freedom of form generation analogous modelling offers – for example in paper folding.

Fig. 3.21 *The thickness and elasticity of the material defines different folding possibilities*

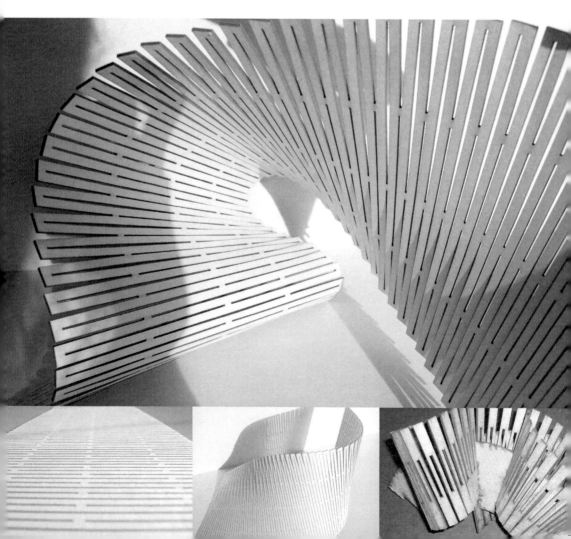

It is also impossible to "feel" the many physical characteristics of the material with this type of digital modelling. At
the same time, it does not mean that digital possibilities are
of secondary importance in the field of modelling. It is precisely the digital techniques that require some experience
in analogue modelling to properly exploit all the potentials
and advantages of these techniques. Using a laser cutter at
this stage, it is possible to cut different lines or curves with
great precision, or even patterns that can be of great help
in this modelling phase. When folding paper, precision can
be achieved by cutting lines on both sides of the paper and
then folding along the lines with great care. Chapter 5 contains more details about the preparation for laser cutting.

While 3D modelling software does not always offer an alternative to the conceptual development through scale
models, it is very important to recognise various software
packages and their capabilities. Depending on the object
complexity, it is necessary to choose the appropriate software that supports a particular concept. If the designed
object was conceived as an object consisting of basic geometric shapes (rectangle, sphere, prism, etc.), then the 3D
modelling is done in simple solid or mesh modelling software (such as SketchUp or AutoCAD). If the designed object was conceived as a free–form object in the conceptual
phase, then modelling should begin in software specialised
for NURBS modelling (Rhinoceros, Maya, etc.). Script languages are often used in very sophisticated tasks, significantly expanding the possibilities for the creation of complex geometric forms.

Working or development scale models are models built during the development of architectural projects or following
the generation of conceptual ideas and models. Working
models are used to develop the basic geometry of architectural projects in which there is at least one more development phase that will occur prior to making the final decision
about the work on white styled models. This phase is used
to work on exchangeable positions of walls, coordination of
proportions and development of different elements. Development scale models increase the level of conceptual models development and focus on the further project development level. These models are often used in consultations
with investors, less frequently with external collaborators
(mainly builders/constructors). They are made quickly, cut
with scissors or scalpel and assembled without the inten-

tion of lasting longer than the very idea they represent. They do not have much detailing and do not have to be perfectly accurate. Working models can be used to explore different aspects of architectural tasks, such as connections between volume, structure, texture or material. This type of model is still an abstract representation of connections within objects and is open for further development. They are still not detailed enough to reflect certain aspects such as wall thickness and materiality. They are therefore still pretty rough in the communication and representation of developing projects. At a certain development level (degree of detailing), these models assume characteristics that open up the possibility of considering their transformation into white styled models.

White styled models are used to present completed conceptual projects. These models should not be mistaken for exhibition scale models that represent the main project stages. White styled models are used to illustrate and confirm design decisions, as well as to communicate with investors who are not entirely familiar with the previous work–studies. These scale models should be detailed enough to demonstrate the best features of objects through the play of light and shadows, where none of the elements (e.g. colour or materialisation) dominate or distract unnecessarily. This type of model is commonly used to present the basic idea and object characteristics to investors, or to those who need to make a decision about its implementation. This type of model is also used in public architectural and city planning contests and competitions (Fig. 3.22).

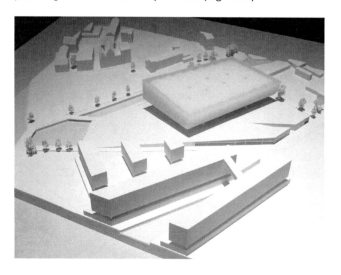

Fig. 3.22 *A competition scale model – Museum of Second World War–Gdanjsk*

Apart from specific analyses, secondary scale models also illustrate the final work on the main project or completed objects, therefore we can divide them into two types: exhibition scale models and scale models of completed structures.

Exhibition scale models, as opposed to white styled models, represent the completion of work on the main project. They are usually built to the same scale as the main project (1:100). However, if objects are large in terms of surface and size, then the scale is smaller (1:200 or 1:250). Exhibition models are made of quality, durable materials, with much more detailing and often finished more realistically. They define many object characteristics and even the context in which structures are positioned (the so–called site scale models), with roads, parking lots, ground floor solutions and landscaping solutions (Fig. 3.23). If objects are placed on inclined lots, then the relevant contour lines are also included. These scale models can also contain other important information, such as: direction of north, wind roses, street or square names, names of typical or important objects in the context of specific areas, if any (e.g. National Theatre), traffic routes, etc. Site models show a reduced version of objects, partly because of the bigger scale in which they are made. Detailing in the presentation of objects viewed in a broader context is limited by scale. Exhibition models are often the last in a series of models made in a project, unless built structures are drastically different from the main project, in which case scale models of completed structures are made instead.

Fig. 3.23 *Exhibition scale model housing complex in Dubai*

Scale models of completed structures are made if planning was not strictly followed during the execution of the main project and the ensuing modifications are clearly visible on the façades, in the structure's form and mass, for example. These models are then made based on the "project of the completed structure", always after the completion of the structure and to supplement the entire project and technical documentation. This is so for several reasons, e.g. functional, technological, economic grounds, but also for reasons relating to the future maintenance of the structure during its lifecycle. Scale models of completed structures are made to quickly find (illustrate) the differences between the designed and completed structures and are often displayed next to exhibition models (if those were respectively made after the completion of main projects, and before the construction of structures), along with information about the type of changes made.

This group of models can include models representing structures of significant architectural heritage or those of protected historical value. They are made to present structures of special importance and to enable detailed and thorough analyses, but also to analyse the parts (details) that are not clearly visible on the actual structure or are hidden by other structures or vegetation of a protected historic unit. These are often archaeological sites, whose aim is also to analyse the bigger picture of the entire complex or its parts, or to indicate the individual, more significant objects within these structures.

3.2.2 Types of scale models according to spatial levels

Scale models discussed here refer to the representation of different spatial levels, and those are scale models of: interior spaces, architectural objects, city planning projects and landscape solutions.

Interior models are made to present studies of the interior space of architectural structures, usually specific public buildings (hospitals, airports, military facilities, etc.) or commercial buildings and offices and rarely of residential buildings. They represent both the architectural space and the furnishings, the planned finishing of surfaces (walls, floors, stairs, etc.), and all important details for interiors, or those needed to make a decision on the adoption of interior de-sign projects. These models give an image of the design, furnishings and the use of materials, colour and lighting in interior spaces. They have defined limits of the visible space to allow observers to see the most interesting and the most characteristic parts of the architectural structure for which the interior design studies are made. These scale models need to be clearly defined and visible. Interior scale models are usually made to the 1:25 scale, which enables realistic treatment of almost every detail of equipment, furniture or walls and floors panelling.

The approach to interior scale modelling is almost the same as that used for architectural scale modelling, since the in-terior designer has to consider the interior space of a struc-ture, its furnishings and treatment, as well as the presenta-tion of the external appearance of the structure itself (the architectural model). The ability to "open the structure" (of-ten by lifting one part of the model, e.g. the roof) and take a look around its interior space (interior) often generates a number of ideas and concepts concerning its furnishings and finishing. Interior models use different visual approach-es to achieve the desired effects in the presentation of inte-rior designer ideas. They can be based on the presentation of the space itself, and most of all, on its furnishings. Realis-tic presentation concepts involve the use of the appropriate (realistic) materials for processing and chosen colours and textures. Today, interior models are often replaced with renderings (computer generated graphics) or interior an-imations that can be "more realistic than reality" and are also cheaper and more applicable in the decision–making process, given that decisions about furnishings come after decisions about the construction.

Architectural scale models are used to present architectur-al projects, which allow for the examination of the form, façade or the different elements, while providing the op-portunity to see the "fifth façade", or take a look at designed structures from the bird's–eye view at the same time. Ar-chitectural scale models are often made separately (de-tached), outside the context in which they are positioned (lots, driveways, parking lots, neighbours, etc.), to examine their form or detailing. These models are usually made in 1:100 scale, or 1:200 for larger buildings. The level of de-tailing depends on the scale. These models are made of different materials, mainly durable materials such as wood, plastic, glass and cardboard. Different materials are often combined when making these models. There are two more types of architectural models that are specific in terms of purpose: façade models (Fig. 3.24) and sectional models.

Façade models are architectural models based on projects, representing only one façade of designed structures. Façade models are made in two cases. The first case is the architectural study of the front façade with one, dominant point of view. Similar studies were typical of the Renaissance period, when the frontal perspective had a major role in the perception of shape and building structure.

Fig. 3.24 *Façade model of an area in Novi Sad, student project, FTN – Architecture, Novi Sad*

Today, this approach is applied to buildings interpolated into urban contexts, with sides touching the sides of other buildings. This usually means building a series of façade models. In fact, these are models of buildings found among other buildings in a street, where viewing the entire building as a detached model is not important for the actual representation of the building itself (its other façades are hidden and cannot be seen because they touch the adjacent buildings). The emphasis of these models is on the appearance of street façades of both the building for which the façade model is made and the frontal view of the entire street. All façades in a street front model should be made to the same scale, while the level of detail may differ (it is recommendable that the newly designed building façade standout from the façades of the existing buildings, either with its level of processing or colour).

Façade models are made with shallow relief of façade elements, thus creating the illusion of larger volume. This type of model is still used for the analysis of streets or traffic in relation to façade cross–sections and height (street profile), which is actually impossible in orthogonal projection. Sectional models are architectural models that are based on projects. They represent cross–sections of designed objects and the correlation between vertical spaces (Fig. 3.25). These models represent cross–sections through relevant and often complex parts, thus permitting the analysis of all the important elements (interior, construction, vertical communication, etc.).

Fig. 3.25 *A sectional model, Museum of Architecture in Stockholm*

Façade sectional models are made at points of interaction between the important functions and elements of structures. They are usually made in those project stages that are more difficult for two–dimensional presentation. These models are often used to analyse details and connections between primarily structural elements. They are often related to interior models, since they also represent the interior space. The main difference between them is vertical orientation, as interior models are typically viewed from above. Sectional models are also closely related to structural (construction) models, whose purpose is to give an overview of the basic structural system.

City models are used to show the broader context (environment) of an architectural structure or to study city planning solutions on a broader level (block, town or city area). Context models are city models made to analyse the correlation between designed objects and their characteristics as well as the mass and characteristics of the existing architecture. They can also be used to show the position and correlation between the existing building (or buildings) and the surrounding blocks, as well as the expansion (development) of one specific city area.

These models incorporate contour models, but they also make possible a number of analyses of city planning and landscaping solutions in relation to a single building. City models most commonly consist of a number of objects in one, usually neutral, colour. Another feature is to leave empty lots in these models where individual scale objects will be inserted later, which is in fact their purpose. These individual (architectural) models are made in the same scale as city models, only more materialised and with more detailing, making them stand out from the other models. When different projects for a particular city area are integrated, objects can be inserted in city models at a later stage (Fig. 3.26). City models often show landscaping solutions too. City models are made to show city planning projects or the existing situation to large numbers of potential users (citizens), as well as to vividly present city projects to the committees that will be approving it. They can be displayed in public places, as an incentive for the established democratic dialogue with potential users (citizens), processors (designers), investors (financial structures) and decision makers (political structures).

Fig. 3.26 *Interpolation into a city model – an example from Hamburg*

City models fully represent the situation and circumstances of city areas they represent, as well as relative city plans. Similar to study models, the purpose of these models is to explore the correlation between individual city elements, only on a much larger scale, given that they illustrate elements of buildings through massive blocks (Fig. 3.27).

Landscape models are built to show city landscaping projects and related features of wider city regions (blocks, districts or areas). These models often represent projects for gardens, the eco–rehabilitation of damaged areas, river banks, lake banks, seashores, etc. Models can represent typical tall vegetation (trees), while shrubs, flower beds and lawns, as well as paving, are presented with visual elements. This depends on the scale, which does not allow too much detailing in some cases (see also Fig. 3.9). Scales of landscape models are identical to the city or architectural model scales. These models, as well as city and architectural models, always represent inclined terrain through different elevation levels of contour lines (provided the terrain is naturally inclined). These models give priority to landscaping and ground floor solutions (ground floor benches, street lamps, pergolas, sculptures, paving, etc.), while architectural structures themselves serve as supplemental elements.

Fig. 3.27 *City model of Hamburg*

The correlation between the landscaping solutions, ground floor plans and architecture is best analysed and viewed precisely through landscape models. The best landscape models are simple and abstract, where the focus is not on the accuracy (realistic presentation using a lot of different materials and colours often gives the impression of kitsch). Landscape models are often made like a collage, which gives free, almost artistic interpretation.

3.2.3   Types of scale models according to structural systems

As defined at the beginning of the chapter, the last general classification of scale models comprises models representing the structural systems of different types of objects. These models are usually made to present structural systems of atypical or complex objects, such as public buildings, stadiums, bridges, etc. Atypical objects are not to be understood as objects whose structural systems are typical and feature complex façades, but those whose structural systems are different from the usual, such as: shells, spatial grid structures, tent structures, etc. Scale models are often made for objects that are structural systems themselves, such as bridges, overpasses and viaducts (especially if they are part of complex spaghetti junctions that are hard to define with drawings). These models are made to a scale of 1:100 to 1: 1000, depending on the requirements and the context for which they are made. They are built of durable materials, mainly wood, polyester and metal.

This group also includes working or construction models of complex structural connections, made in a much larger scale, even 1:1 or larger. This primarily means construction of models representing the connections between reinforcement elements or relevant complex formwork. These models are usually made of wood and wire and have no lasting value, except to show drawings to contractors on site.

All models require bearing systems, usually depending on the geometry of the form, the end purpose of objects and the purpose of models. In terms of architecture education, building scale models with different types of bearing systems is the first step towards the students' understanding of statics principles and problems, where learning–by–doing methods help them solve problems. Scale model bearing systems depend on the construction methods, i.e. whether models are made manually or digitally. Depending on their construction and making, models can be divided into physical and digital models. Physical models are assembled from individual parts that can be cut manually or with laser cutters. The bearing systems of these models can match the bearing systems of designed objects, or they can have their own independent structural systems. In terms of bearing systems, physical models can be divided into the following groups:

- Scale models with massive (solid) bearing systems,

- Scale models with planar bearing systems,

- Scale models with linear bearing systems,

- Thin–shell structures

Models with **massive (solid) bearing** systems are very stable. These models can be made of solid blocks of material (e.g. XPS, EPS) or stacked surface materials that provide the desired thickness (plywood, cardboard or plexiglass). Massive materials are materials whose three basic dimensions (length, width and thickness) are approximately the same. The basic construction principle of these models is cutting or shaping the basic materials to achieve the desired form, which is similar to sculpting. On the other hand, massive (solid) bearing systems require specific building techniques when surface materials are used. With these models, objects are divided into horizontal segments – sections – in intervals depending on material thickness (Fig. 3.28).

Fig. 3.28 *An example of two objects with different types of massive bearing system*

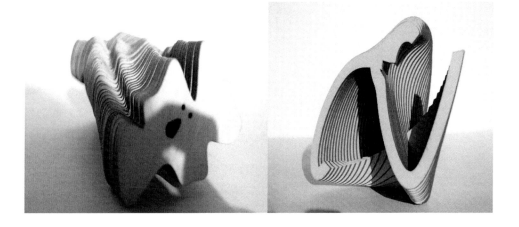

Object contours are cut based on these sections and then affixed to one another. Of course, depending on object types, sections can also be vertical. The figure on the left shows all horizontal sections in full form, while the sections of the object on the right were cut in the shape of a ring. Significant material savings are possible this way. These models are usually made for terrain or free–form objects. Fig. 3.29 shows a model with a massive (solid) system that was made brick by brick, just like the original structure.

Fig. 3.29 A scale model at the exhibition "Re–Sampling Ornament", 2009

Models with **planar bearing systems** are mostly used in modelmaking (Fig. 3.30). These models are made of paper, cardboard, plexiglass, etc. The main characteristic of these materials is that two dimensions of the material, length and width, are significantly larger than the material thickness.

Fig. 3.30 A scale model with the surface bearing system

is developed in the shape of a grid and the grid is then cut out in the desired material. Given that only two–dimensional materials are used with this type of models (the third dimension is significantly smaller than the first two), it is impossible to make double curved surfaces.

Models with **linear systems** are made of elements whose third dimension is significantly smaller than the first two dimensions (Fig. 3.31).

Fig. 3.31 *A detail of a linear bearing system model*

Due to the assembly process itself, these models are much more sensitive, since the connection systems between the linear elements are quite unstable in nature. Individual elements can be equipped with rollers or plastic balls in this case. Scale models with linear systems are particularly important for models with double–curved surfaces, which is when linear elements are given the structural function of beams in two directions. This principle is used extensively in the making of models of digitally generated forms that have complex structures with double–curved surfaces. Free surface cross–sections are made with software tools used in two directions. Cross–section lines generate the bearing structures or two–directional support beams. Apart from defining linear structural elements, this principle can be used to define the surface layer lines with geodesic lines.

Thin–shell structures are spatial structures made of shell elements, curved surface elements whose thickness is negligibly small compared to the other two dimensions. A separate group of thin–shell structures are membrane structures, with in–plane tension loads only (Fig. 3.32).

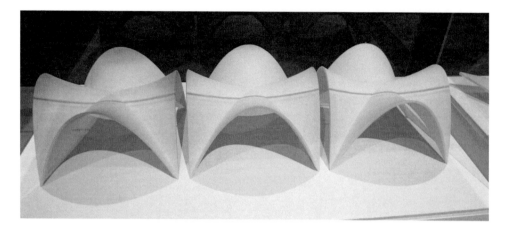

In the sixties and seventies, scale models played a key role in the study of free–form shell structures. The analogue approach to thin shell structure research required simultaneous monitoring of conceptual physical models and load–test models, with strain gauges and load measurements (Fig. 3.33). New digital design technologies incorporating the FEA (Finite Element Analysis) method have triggered a new revolution in the study of form, allowing relaxing (with dynamic relaxation method) any mesh into a stressed surface in equilibrium with positive stress fields only.

Fig. 3.32 Scale models of membrane structures, Felix Candela, Parroquia de San Antonio de las Huertas, Miguel Hidalgo, Mexixo 2012, Nylon SLS

Digital scale models are printed with 3D printers or made so that the process ends in a single integral scale model (Fig. 3.34). Of course, depending on the size of models and 3D printers, more than one printed section can be assembled into a single large model.

Fig. 3.33 Load–test model of membrane structures, Heinz Isler, 13th International Architecture Exhibition – Common Graund, Venice, 2012

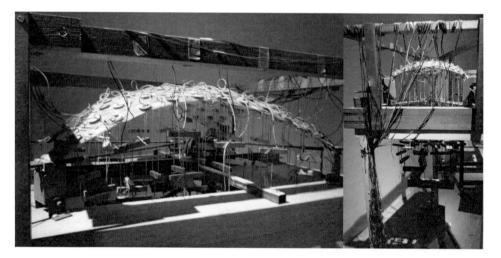

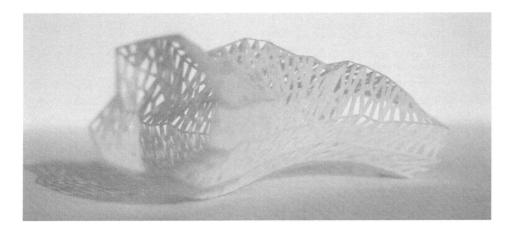

The assembling of parts in this context is not the same as structural assembling. It is simply the "alignment of parts" into a larger unit. 3D printers can also print individual segments that are then assembled into a single model (Fig. 3.35).Digital fabrication of scale models with 3D printers can be divided into two groups:

Fig. 3.34 *A scale model printed on a 3D printer*

– Fabrication of solid models, and

– Fabrication of surface models.

The basic difference between these two systems, regardless of the object form, is this: fabrication of solid models means that the entire model volume is filled with material (Fig. 3.36 left). With surface models, on the other hand, only the surface is made of solid materials, while their interior is hollow (Fig. 3.36 right).

Fig. 3.35 *Individual detailing segments assembled into a single unit*

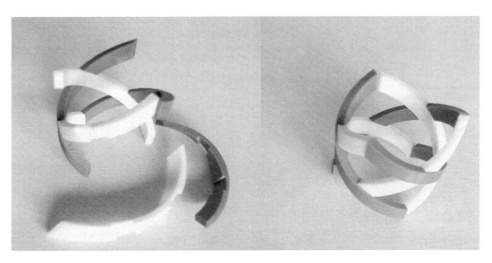

Depending on geometric forms of objects to be printed, the type of 3D printers and used materials, there are limitations that need to be understood in the early stages of digital modelling. More about the limitations and specifics of different printing methods will be discussed in Chapter 6.2.2.

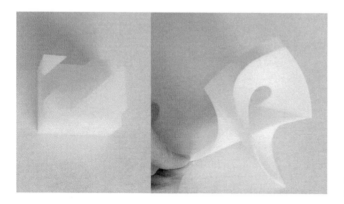

Fig. 3.36 A solid model and a hollow – surface model

With the help of CNC machines or robot arms, it is possible to produce massive models made of volumetric materials (XPS, EPS or wood). This method requires CNC machines to eliminate the unnecessary parts of materials by milling them to the desired level. The method is very useful for models with irregular geometric structures, such as the terrain model shown in Fig. 3.37. This method can also be used for fabrication of objects with non–standard structures and curved surfaces in real size. In this case digital models are divided into segments whose size depends on the size of the standard material of XPS panels.

Fig. 3.37 Terrain model made with a CNC machine

Each segment is individually processed with a CNC machine, and then the individual parts are affixed, sanded and coated with final protective coatings (Fig. 3.38 and Fig. 3.39).

Fig. 3.38 Fabrication in the project "Ideal House" by Zaha Hadid

Fig. 3.39 Scale Model of Heydar Aliyev Centre, Baku, Azerbaijan, arch. Zaha Hadid, 13th International Architecture Exhibition – Common Graund, Venice, 2012

3.3   Scale

As mentioned in previous chapters and explained by individual examples, scale models are built in different scales. Choosing the appropriate scale prior to the beginning of work on a model, depends on many conditions. Scales differ depending on the type of models and the purpose of their representation of objects and their physical sizes. Some objects can be made as scale models in large or small scale, depending on the purpose and needs of representation.

The selection of scale for scale models generally depends on the physical or actual size of objects (as well as location/ lot on which objects are located) they are going to represent. Scale also depends on the size of the workspace that models can/will require. Selection of scale also depends on the project stage that is to be illustrated with scale models (study models, working models or exhibition models). The next requirement for the selection of scale is the level of detailing that is to be presented, from working/conceptual models and white styled models to detail and interior models. Therefore, by reducing the scale of models their visible level of detailing is increased, while an increase of their scale decreases the level of detailing to the level of geometric primitives (architectural block forms). This is why it is more adequate and practical to make smaller models for the understanding of fine detailing, rather than larger ones with insufficient detailing.

There are also models that are not made in specific scales. These are commonly conceptual, development models whose scale can be subsequently "added" (calculated), after they have already been made and approved. This mainly applies to models built to a quality acceptable for the next project stage and development of basic ideas presented with scale models. This principle is applied to preserve the models, so that they do need to be built again in a specific scale at a later stage. This practice, of course, does not have any strict rules, and the subsequent calculation of scale is necessary because of the copying of the dimensions of the final form of such models, which is then incorporated into the project for further elaboration.

If during the construction of models additional standard furnishing elements are used (such as landscaping solutions and people), one must keep in mind that ready–made elements like these can be bought in specific scales only (1:10, 1:20, 1:100 or 1: 200). If these elements are built manually, then scale is not a limiting factor.

During the design and construction of scale models, it is necessary to consider the correlation between different architectural and urban elements and the size of the human figure. This includes the range of very small objects such as details or connections, to very large ones such as cities or landscapes. What is important in all situations is to understand and control the proportions of space and its elements by direct positioning into the context of proportions of the human figure, all in the control context of the building.

The understanding of scale does not mean that all reasoning is related to the proportions of the human body. Space can actually be understood from the aspect of human perception only through the study of spatial relationships. There are many examples of relationships between different scales, out of which we are giving a few here: the relationship between

−   the relationship between the human body and the scale of a room,

−   the relationship between a room and the scale of the whole building,

−   the relationship between a building and the scale of a block and

−   the relationship between a block and the size of an entire city.

To easily identify the frame of reference for the construction of scale models, the table below gives the types of scale models with the appropriate scales.

In addition to the mentioned scales, they are sometimes built in different scales because some countries still use a non–metric system of measurements (e.g. the United States), such as 1:24 for interior models, 1:160 and 1:240 for architectural models and 1:480 and 1:1200 for city models.

In any case, the art of being able to perceive the appropriate scale whose basic module is the human figure, is important for the coordination of all elements built in the particular space. The more harmonious the coordination of the relationships between built elements, the more humane the space in which people live and work will be. From the scale model point of view, all this experience, knowledge and sensibility has to be instilled in it (Table 3.1).

Type of scale model	Scale
Detail model	2:1 or 1:1
Interior/Furniture model	1:25
Conceptual/ Development model	1:50, 1:100, 1:200 or with no specific scale
Exhibition model, model of constructed objects	
- small volume	1:100
- large volume	1:200
Site model	1:250 or 1:500
City/Landscape model	
- small environment	1:250 or 1:500
- broad environment	1:1000 or 1:2500

Table 3.1 *Type of scale models*

The following, fourth chapter of this book discusses all the required tools, accessories and different materials, which will contribute to a better understanding of the materialisation options of different types of models.

References:

[1]   Ansgar, O.: Meister der Miniaturen Architektur Modelbau. DOM publishers, Berlin (2008)

[2]   Dunn, N.: Come realizzare un modelo architettonico. Logos, Modena, (2010)

[3]   Institute for Architecture and Media: https://iam2.tugraz.at/fwf/freeform/, Accessed 6 August 2012

[4]   Knoll, W., Hechinger, M.: Architektur – modelle Anregungrn zu ihrem Bau. Deutsche Verlags –Anstalt, München (2006)

[5]   Mills B. C.: Designing with models – A Studio Guide to Making and Using Architectural Design Models. John Wiley & Sons, Inc. Hoboken, New Jersey (2005)

[6]   Šiđanin, P., Tepavčević, B.: Maketarstvo za studente arhitekture. FTN, Novi Sad, (2010)

4 MODELLING TOOLS AND MATERIALS

4 MODELLING TOOLS AND MATERIALS

The art and practice of scale modelling have changed significantly with digital technology. The application of laser cutters and CNC milling machines has made the cutting stage
considerably easier; 3D printers are now used to realise architectural and other scale models, which has facilitated the
process of fabrication. This has influenced both the speed
and precision of model building. At the same time, digital
techniques and 3D CAD software have made the geometry
of designs increasingly complex. Scale models are thus built
to inspect or test the individual elements of designs; on the
other hand, they have likewise become more complex and
challenging to manufacture. Despite all the digital possibilities at hand, manual tools are still used in the traditional
way. Hence, this chapter provides an overview of both the
digital and traditional modelling tools and materials.

Depending on their purpose, scale models are made in different size ratios and may show more or less detail, as discussed in the chapter 3. Also, they are built from a variety of
materials relative to their size, intended use and desired effects. Depending on the selected materials, special tools are
used. In this chapter we present the basic kit and materials
used to manufacture different kinds of scale models and
touch upon some properties of new types of paint which
may be used to good advantage in scale modelling today.

4.1   Modelling Tools

To be properly equipped, any professional modelling studio
or workshop should have the basic tools needed to process
a range of materials. The fabrication tools used for material processing/cutting may be divided into analogue and
digital. Those most commonly used by model makers are

laser cutters, CNC milling machines and 3D printers. Over the last few years, industrial robots have found increasing applications in the manufacturing not only of scale models, but also of architectural elements, opening a new chapter in their fabrication. A detailed assessment of the upsides and downsides of digital fabrication tools is given in Chapter 4.3 and in part of the Tutorial.

Unlike digital tools with digitally programmed/controlled cutting and processing functions, analogue tools are tools in the traditional sense of the word (drills, saws, etc.). The tools must be high–quality ones, whose reliability and dura-bility ensure the manufacturing of even the most demand-ing scale models. The majority of tools manufactured today have interchangeable parts and can be used to process var-ious materials or for special processing purposes, allowing a single tool to be used to manufacture many different scale model components. The traditional tools may be classified into several groups:

—   cutting tools,
—   drilling tools,
—   processing tools,
—   painting tools, and
—   accessories.

Cutting tools are different kinds of saws, such as circular saws and jigsaws (Fig. 4.1), which are used for the initial processing of scale model components, which are fine–fin-ished in the subsequent phases. Circular saws may be large and heavy, requiring a permanent position in the workshop and plenty of operating space; also, they need constant stable power supply. Saws may be table–mounted, with feeds, a ventilator, a filter and a dust/sawdust extraction bag. They may also be hand–held and human–powered or electric, and are used to process wood and other materials in different ways. Along with the common types of saws, there are jigsaws which are specially used to cut openings in boards as well as to make irregular, circular or undulating edges (e.g., contours).

There are many different types of hand–held saws, and they are all used for special ways of cutting or with particular materials. Also, there are small–size fine–finish saws with specially suited blades used for the final processing of work-pieces.

Fig. 4.1 Cutting tools – a jig saw and a special circular saw used by model builders

Most saws have interchangeable blades and may be used to cut a range of materials and to perform different cutting functions.

There are also other cutting tools, such as cutting chisels with hammers (iron, rubber or wooden), scissors or shears (for metal, plastics and paper) and various special cutters.

Drilling tools are different kinds of drills (Fig. 4.2). Drills may be bench– or table–mounted, when their size and weight require that they be fixed permanently in the workshop. They are used for drilling materials of various types and thicknesses. Also, they may be adjusted in a number of ways and are highly flexible to operate. Stationary drills are used for precision drilling as they allow the fastening and marking of even the smallest components.

Fig. 4.2 Drilling tools – a traditional drill and a mini drill press

Special drill bits of varying diameters are used with different materials to avoid damaging the surface of the material during drilling. Apart from these, hand–held drills are also used. The latter are mainly electricity–powered, but there are also human–powered drills, which are used for fine–finishing small workpieces.

Computer–controlled cutting machines rely on digital input parameters for operation, i.e., for processing and/or cutting materials. Laser cutters cut via a laser beam, either by drilling or engraving a material. A variety of materials may be cut and engraved with laser cutters, depending on their power and speed. The preparation of digital files for laser cutting involves making 2D drawings using CAD, based on which the laser head receives input on how to move in the x and y directions, as well as on the speed and power of the beam needed to perform particular cutting functions. The materials cut with laser cutters range from paper and cardboard to acrylic glass and hardboard. Fabricating replicas of complex non–standard buildings or structures has become virtually impossible without laser cutters, which makes them a must–have for any modelling workshop. In general, laser–cut components do not require fine–finishing and may be immediately joined together in the final scale model. CNC milling machines are also used to cut a range of materials. When preparing digital input for CNC machining, one must take into account the diametre of the bit that will do the cutting, as the radius of each internal angle of the manufactured components will equal the bit radius. In some cases, the model fabrication may require the use of non–standard materials, e.g. steel or marble, in which case CNC technologies other than laser cutters are used (e.g., water jet cutters).

Finishing tools and machines are various kinds of planes, lathes, etc. used for fine–finishing workpieces (Fig. 4.3). Each of these tools may be a separate machine that needs its own work space. Electric planes or grinders are used to remove layers of wood, and when fitted with special blades or other attachments, they can also be used to mould components. These tools come with an assortment of removable blades (with flat, slant or contoured edges). Machine tools/lathes are special devices used for turning, i.e., producing rotational parts. They are stationary and of relatively large, cumbersome size, and are used to process wood and metal. Operating machine tools usually requires a brief period of training and some experience.

Fig. 4.3 Various kinds of
grinding bits used for fine–
finishing

Fine–finishing tools are commonly used to file/sand or grind
the surface or edges of a workpiece, and come in the form
of abrasive paper, plates and wheels. They are removable
and are usually fitted into a hand–held drill. Removable
sandpaper sheets come in various grit sizes. There are also
grinding bits of different shapes, which are used depending
on the workpiece that needs fine–finishing.

Painting tools are devices made up of a number of components (Fig. 4.4). Painting the entire model or the materials used for building individual components smoothly and
consistently requires the use of a special spray booth. By
working in a spray booth one avoids smearing or spraying
the workshop or work space with paint. Air compressors are
the basic painting tools used in scale modelling. Depending
on the painting needs, air compressors of various transfer
efficiencies (volume to pressure ratio) are used. An air compressor is used with a range of accessories, such as a spray
gun with an adjustable nozzle, a paint tank with a suction
cup of varying capacity, an air hose, and a gauge complete
with a rubber guard. Air compressors often come with interchangeable air dusters, used to dust entire models or individual model components. Wearing protective gear, which
includes a face mask (covering both the nose and eyes),
gloves and overalls, is obligatory when working with paint
and air compressors. There are also mini air compressors,
which may be obtained from well–stocked toy shops. These
mini air compressors usually come with interchangeable
compressed air cylinders, which basically atomise the paint
to allow its application.

Fig. 4.4 *Mini air compressor used in scale modelling*

4.2   Modelling Kit

Other tools are also used by model builders. Principally, the tools used in scale modelling may be divided into the basic toolkit and accessories, an overview of which is given below, with a brief explanation on how they are used.

4.2.1   Basic Kit

The main tools used in scale modelling are very simple, easy to find, inexpensive, and they meet most of the model builder's needs. Some of these tools may also be replaced with others that are simpler or easier to obtain.

Drawing tools may be digital or analogue. The term "digital drawing tools" refers to using CAD software to prepare files to transfer to the laser cutter, and by 'analogue tools" we mean traditional drawing tools.

Drawing tools are the basic tools used to draw the main components of the scale model (Fig. 4.5). These components, which are meant to represent an actual building once they are assembled, are scaled down directly or by calculating their size based on the building specifications, and then transferred onto the material from which they are cut. The drawing kit contains t–squares, rulers, protractors, French curves, various templates, etc., all the tools used traditionally to make analogue architectural drawings.

A variety of CAD software is currently available on the market that may be used to export files for laser cutting. The size of the material to be cut by the laser cutter will vary depending on the size of the cutter. Laser cutters may be used to engrave raster images, extending the range of applications of the laser technology. When using CAD to make drawings, it is important to know the thickness of the material that will be cut in advance, which should be factored in when sizing adjoining elements. Double lines on drawings must be avoided; as well as that, it is necessary to test the laser power on a sample of the material before cutting the components and adjust the speed to cut them to the specified dimensions. Although there are many advantages in using digital instead of analogue tools when drawing and cutting conceptual and working models (or when adjusting or making corrections to already existing models), it is sometimes easier and more appropriate to use traditional tools. Traditional drawing tools are discussed in greater detail in the text below for this reason.

Cutting boards are made of vinyl and used to protect the surface of the desk/drawing board when cutting with a touch knife or scalpel. These boards have stamped rasters on them, which are usually orthogonal, to help cutting. They vary in size and may be purchased in well–stocked model or arts and crafts shops. Thick and hard paperboard may be used instead of a cutting board.

Fig. 4.5 *Basic drawing tools and a cutting board*

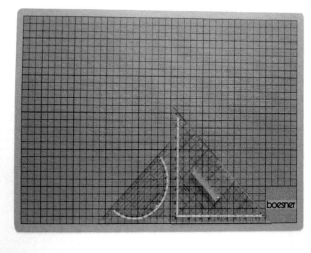

Aluminium/metal rulers and t–squares serve as guides when cutting straight lines with a scalpel (cutter). They are used instead of plastic or wooden rulers and t–squares, whose guides may easily be damaged during cutting. Unlike them, the edges of metal tools are much more difficult to damage. Like plastic and wooden tools, metal rulers and t–squares are graduated in centimetres (or other scales). These tools do not slide thanks to a non–skid rubber backing, which makes them highly convenient as it keeps the scalpel from straying. Ordinary rulers and t–squares made of plastic or wood may be used instead of metal tools; however, when damaged, they should be replaced with new ones.

Cutting knives or scalpels are some of the most important modelling tools and they must be selected with great care. One should always choose knives with interchangeable or breakable press–fit blades (those which cannot move freely during the cutting). There are different types of modelling knives, but the most commonly used are touch knives with disposable sliding blades (Fig. 4.6). This type of knife has a steel blade with break–off notches along its length. Once the blade has become blunt, it may be broken off along the notch nearest the tip, by placing it into the slit in the re-movable handle end designed and used specifically for this purpose. Touch knives are sold with spare blades, which may also be purchased separately, and which are kept in a plastic box. These modelling or hobby knives are used for both rectilinear cutting and cutting along free–form lines (curves). When it is not being used, the blade of a touch knife should be pulled inside the handle to avoid injury.

Fig. 4.6 *Cutting tools and disposable touch knife blades*

Another type of cutting tool used in scale modelling are scalpels with interchangeable blades (Fig. 4.7). These scalpels have handles made of metal or plastic and are used with unbreakable blades. The blades, which may be removed from the handle, are made in various shapes. Different blades are used with different materials and for different cutting purposes. These scalpels are most often used to cut out openings (doors and windows). They are specialised tools and are much more expensive than touch knives. They are used to cut both rectilinear and curvilinear shapes. Since they have very sharp blades, these tools should be kept in protective cases when not used to avoid injury.

Fig. 4.7 Scalpel with a set of interchangeable blades

The third type of cutter is the mount scalpel, which may be used to cut at an angle of 45° (Fig. 4.8). Mount scalpels are very useful when cutting components that will be joined at right angles. To cut with them, they should be set against the ruler guide and moved along it. Mount scalpels are used for cutting only rectilinear shapes. They have very sharp replaceable blades, which should be pulled inside the handle when not used to avoid accidental injury.

Fig. 4.8 Scalpel for cutting at an angle of 45°

Hot–wire foam cutters also belong in the cutting toolkit used by model builders (Fig. 4.9). They may be of various types, shapes and sizes and are used to cut styrofoam and other lightweight plastic foam materials. To use this tool, it is connected to the mains through a transformer, and when the wire has become hot, it is pressed against the material to melt it. It takes a lot of experience to get a straight or a free–form cut with hot wire. Very interesting irregular shapes may be cut with hot wire tensioned with a bow or attached to a rigid frame. Guides and tables or stands are often used with hot–wire cutters to make the cutting easier. The wire is heated to very high temperatures to be able to cut through a material, so caution is recommended when using it and protective gloves should be worn to avoid accidental injury.

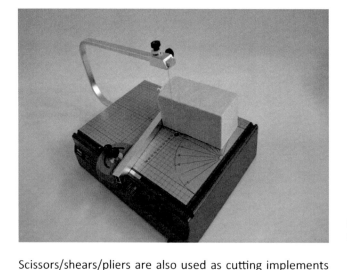

Fig. 4.9 *Table–mounted hot–wire foam cutter*

Scissors/shears/pliers are also used as cutting implements (Fig. 4.10). There are scissors/shears of various shapes, sizes and blades, which are used with different materials. Scissors are used in scale modelling to cut thin materials or to produce makeshift studio models from paper or thin paperboard. Except for paper–cutting scissors, there are shears used to cut metal, mainly sheet metal and wire. While there are different types of metal–cutting shears, only those comparatively small in size have applications in scale modelling. Pliers are used to hold workpieces during processing and to cut thin wire. Different kinds of pliers are used for different purposes, but there are some which are used exclusively for cutting wire.

Fig. 4.10 Different kinds of pliers for cutting and holding workpieces

Sandpaper and files are tools used to process/finish wooden and metal workpieces (Fig. 4.11). Special types of sandpaper are used with wood, metal and stone, made of different kinds of backing (usually heavy paper) coated with abrasive particles of different kinds and sizes. Metal sandpaper is typically black in colour, and that used with wood or stone may be ochre, green, red or black. These different kinds are all used in the same way. Sandpaper is both flexible and stiff, and it is easy to tear or cut (it should never be cut with scissors, but with a touch knife or scalpel, and always across the backing).

Fig. 4.11 Sandpaper of different types and grit sizes

Every piece or strip of sandpaper has the type and grit size marks printed on the backing. An accessory tool is often made of wood, polystyrene foam or paperboard on which sandpaper is stuck or fixed, making it easier to work with. Files may be used along with sandpaper. There are different types of files for wood, metal and plastics, ranging from very large to very small, with rough teeth to dead smooth ones. Files may have different cross–sections and are used to process even the finest, most delicate workpieces, including those requiring special treatment (e.g., circular openings with small cross–sections), which are otherwise impossible to finish (e.g., with sandpaper).

The assembly kit may contain different kinds of gripping tools such as pliers, snips and tweezers (Fig. 4.12). Pliers, usually small in size and of different shapes, limb lengths and jaws (flat–nose, narrow flat–nose, round–nose, curved round–nose, etc.), are used to hold workpieces gently while gluing them together.

Tweezers are used instead of pliers when working with thin materials which require great precision or when joining not easily accessible workpieces. Tweezers of various shapes, lengths of legs and jaws are used according to need. The assembly kit may contain metal or wood angle bars or braces, which help to join together workpieces at right angles. As needed, makeshift angle bars or braces at other angles may be made of wood or thick strong paperboard.

Fig. 4.12 *Gripping tools*

Different kinds of adhesives are used in scale modelling (Fig. 4.13). Adhesive tape is certainly the main type of adhesive used to put together makeshift studio models made of paper. It may also be used for other purposes and with other types of models. There are many types of adhesive tape, and the type used on the scale model should not leave traces of the adhesive coating on the material or damage it upon removal, i.e., it must be easy to remove. The type of adhesive most commonly used by model builders is universal glue, which may be used to bond together different materials and is sold in tubes, bottles or other packaging with a tip or mouth that allows thin–coat application. Other glues are sometimes used, such as two–component adhesives, polyvinyl acetate adhesives and various special glues. These types of adhesives are used with materials which may not be stuck together using standard or universal glues. Spray adhesives are used to glue transparent foil and plastic masses. Wooden materials are best glued with special wood adhesives. When using adhesives in scale modelling, it is very advisable to test each new material that needs to be bonded to another material. The test shows the adhesive properties of the glue, i.e., if it will bite into, burn or damage the surface of the material on which it is applied, as well as its durability. These tests should be performed on small samples of the material(s) used, and based on the results one should decide which materials will be glued using which adhesives, i.e., which type of adhesive should be applied on each of the materials.

Fig. 4.13 Various adhesives

One should also bear in mind that there are adhesives which change colour when dry; e.g., wood glue is white and milky, but it becomes transparent after curing. Also, there are adhesives which are glossy on application and become matte as they dry. On the whole, most glues change the colour intensity of the surface they are applied to. One must remember all this before bonding different materials/workpieces together.

Nails are not often used in scale modelling. As a rule, they are used to join the rough, wooden components of the model and must thus be thin and made of brass or steel (pins are sometimes used instead). Nails are used only in those situations and at places/on surfaces where they will remain hidden on the completed scale model.

Protective clothing comprises gloves (cotton, leather or rubber), safety goggles and face masks (Fig. 4.14). It is worn in special situations, when using certain materials and tools may injure parts of the body, which is why they must be protected adequately. Light cotton gloves (white) are used for protection in order not to dirty the completed model when moving it. Latex gloves are most often used as hand protection when painting the model. Safety goggles are worn when operating lathes, planes and other tools used to remove material particles (e.g., sawdust) that may get inside one's eyes and injure them. They are used together with the face mask, which is obligatory when spray painting. Special shields are used for welding operations, which protect both the eyes and face.

Fig. 4.14 *Protective gear/ clothing*

4.2.2 Accessories

Accessory tools are all those tools which may be used in scale modelling, usually for special purposes. Such tools facilitate the building of a scale model, but it is nonetheless possible to make excellent models without using them.

Rotary cutters ("pizza slicers") are used to cut curved lines in thin materials (Fig. 4.15). These cutters have circular knives of different types, from those cutting uninterrupted lines to broken lines to dotted perforations. They are not frequently used in scale modelling, as model builders mainly use touch knives or scalpels instead.

Fig. 4.15 Rotary cutter

Plastic cutters or scribers are special implements used for cutting thin sheet plastic (Fig. 4.16). To cut a plastic sheet with a scriber, the sheet is scored repeatedly to remove layers of the material until it has been cut through.

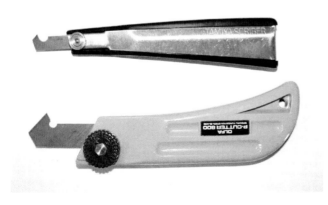

Fig. 4.16 Plastic scribers

Wood carving knives are usually sold in sets of tools of different shapes (Fig. 4.17). They are used to carve and remove layers of wood, by pressing the knife handle with the hand or hitting it gently with a rubber hammer. They are used for fine woodwork and wood carving.

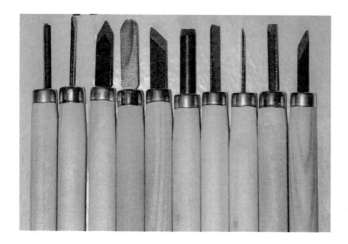

Fig. 4.17 Wood carving knives

Clay tools also come in sets of several utensils (Fig. 4.18). A clay tool consists of a wooden handle (it may also be metal) and a shaped piece of steel wire attached at its end. These shapes are used for modelling clay. Apart from these, there are also solid wooden tools for clay cutting and modelling, as well as tin tools of various shapes used for the same purpose. A mitre box is a small–size tool used to cut sticks, poles and bars at 45– and 90–degree angles (Fig. 4.19).

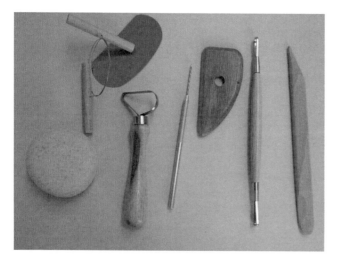

Fig. 4.18 Clay tools

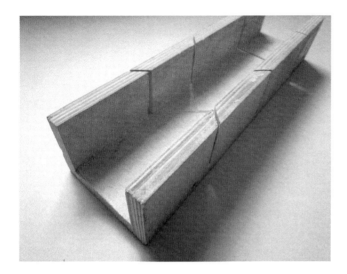

Fig. 4.19 Small–size mitre box

Hot glue guns may be used to bond workpieces together, which they do by melting plastic sticks (Fig. 4.20). This gluing method is considered very reliable. Hot glue guns are sold in different sizes, depending on the application precision requirements.

A "third hand" is a tool employed to assist when gluing and drying workpieces that are difficult to access or manipulate (Fig. 4.21). Instead of using a "third hand", the model builder may use the assistance of a real helping hand to hold the workpieces.

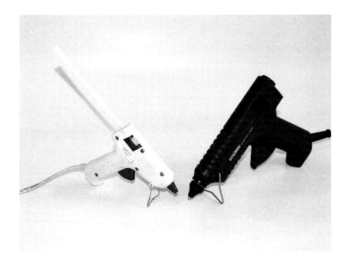

Fig. 4.20 Hot glue guns of different sizes

Fig. 4.21 "Third hand" tool

A soldering iron is an accessory hand tool used for soldering wire (Fig. 4.22). Although it is used only rarely, it is still a useful tool and most modelling studios and workshops keep it in their inventory.

Fig. 4.22 Soldering iron

Gas dusters, which are sold in specialised shops, are used for cleaning workpieces with compressed gas. They come in cans with nozzles with a flexible extension that may reach even the most inaccessible parts of the scale model. Pressing the nozzle at the top of the can activates the compressed gas which dusts the model. Compressed air blow guns may be used instead of gas dusters.

Paint tools consist of brushes, small sponges, paint and diluents, as needed (Fig. 4.23).

Fig. 4.23 Paint tools (brushes) and a can of spray paint

Acrylic paint is used most frequently because it is diluted with water and extremely durable. Painting the scale model can be an intricate task and should thus be carefully planned, prepared and executed. Different types of paint and painting methods are used with different materials.

Spray paint or aerosol paint is often used to paint parts of the scale model, and sometimes for the entire model. Working with spray paint takes a lot of experience, without which the entire model can easily be ruined. A lack of experience in using spray paint may result in uncontrolled application, splattering, overspreading, material swelling, etc. Stencils/ templates or protective tape are often used when working with spray paint. This type of paint is generally nitro–based and as such it is hazardous to human health when applied indoors. As scale models are typically built indoors, it is recommended to use water–based spray paint and keep the room ventilated throughout the painting process.

Self–adhesive tape is used to mark off those parts of the model that need to be painted and to protect the adjoining pieces or surfaces from becoming smeared with paint (Fig. 4.24). There are different kinds of self–adhesive tape, which mostly differ in width. There is also double–sided adhesive tape, which is tacky on both sides. Double–sided adhesive tape is used as an aid when fixing or joining workpieces together.

Fig. 4.24 Adhesive tape

Other hand tools are all those tools acquired or produced by model builders over time; quite often, they are tools remodelled or readjusted to meet special needs. These are mostly metal templates, cutting guides (for curvilinear cutting), sandpaper holders, clamps of different sizes, etc.

Accessories also include the items needed to keep the modelling workshop/studio clean and tidy. Every workshop should be immaculate, and its tools and accessories adequately maintained, cleaned and kept in their proper places. The vacuum cleaner is most certainly one of the basic appliances used to keep the working space clean both during and after work. Vacuum cleaners are used to remove coarse and fine dirt, both wet and dry. Since scale modelling entails a variety of operations, the vacuum cleaner should be strong, stable, easy to move, of large capacity and universal (wet/dry vacuuming). Along with the vacuum cleaner, the cleaning kit comprises other items for cleaning (various brooms and brushes, dustpans, bags, etc.), washing (cloths, buckets, mops, etc.), and various cleansers. The cleaning kit should be kept in a special room or in a secluded part of the workshop, together with the modelling materials.

Finally, because various tools and materials are used in modelling studios/workshops, they are at risk of catching fire and must be protected accordingly. Thus, every professional modelling studio or workshop needs to be equipped with fire extinguishers. They come in various types and sizes and should be procured based on the size and range of operations performed at the workshop. This also helps decide on the type and number of the fire extinguishers needed, as well as the places where they should be kept. A fire risk assessment company ought to be hired to assess the fire risk, and the fire extinguishers must be easily accessible and kept in their designated places at all times.

4.3   Modelling Materials

In this chapter we present and discuss some of the materials used in architectural scale modelling. There are various materials that can be chosen from and a number of aspects should be considered before selecting the main material for the scale model [1],[5],[6],[9]. These aspects are: the time needed to realise the model (there is often a deadline to be met), the level of modification and permissible experimentation (alternative solutions), the potential of the material to be modelled to match or correspond to the design (e.g., achieving the required curvature), or the thickness of the material needed to make the components to the specified scale (e.g., building a wall/column of the required thickness/diametre).

Materials may be classified in groups according to their properties or how they are marketed (packed for sale). Both these classification criteria are relevant because of the possibilities and ways in which materials can be used, and for the purpose of their adequate storage and protection. Material storage refers to keeping materials in a proper place in the modelling studio or workshop, i.e., indoors and in a clean area, not outdoors or under eaves or a cover.

Materials are classified as sheet materials, linear materials, volumetric materials, materials used for modelling amorphous shapes, "smart" or "intelligent" materials, and additional materials according to their basic properties.

4.3.1   Sheet Materials

By definition, a sheet material is any material with a specified, mainly standard length (a) to width (b) ratio, whose thickness (c) is negligible. Common sheet materials are paper and paperboard, various kinds of veneer and wooden panels, natural cork, polystyrene, plastic foil, glass and sheet metal. Depending on how rigid they are, materials are marketed either as rolls or as horizontally or vertically packed sheets, and are well protected from damage. Thin materials are stored horizontally, whereas glass panels and thick sheet materials may be stored vertically. These materials are used to make rigid plane elements, such as facets and panels, as well as folding or deployable systems, tessellation patterns and developable surfaces, like flat–foldable surfaces and rigid foldable origami. If a material will be laser–cut, special attention must be paid to how it is stored, as folded or crumpled material (esp. paper) will impact the quality of the cut. As the laser beam is focused relative to the material surface, a folded or crumpled sheet (of paper or another material) will obstruct the beam, resulting in an interrupted or very broad cut, which can spoil the scale model.

Paper is certainly the most commonly used sheet material (Fig. 4.25). It is made from paper/paperboard pulp and comes in a range of basis weights, textures, colours, sizing, types, etc. Paper and paperboard are produced and marketed in the form of sheets of various standard sizing and basis weights, or in the form of rolls. There are special kinds of paper for various uses, mainly in the art and printing industries (e.g., watercolour paper, onionskin paper, tracing paper, cartridge paper, coated paper, etc.). Nearly all kinds of paper may be used to build scale models. Paperboard is thicker than ordinary paper and is also marketed as various products (e.g., cardboard, Triplex, Passepartout, etc.).

Fig. 4.25 *Different types of paperboard*

Passepartout is particularly popular amongst model builders because it is thick and easy to cut. Paper is cut with
scissors or touch knives/scalpels and glued with paper adhesive. Likewise, paperboard is cut with scalpels and glued
with paper or wood adhesive. Paper and paperboard are
highly flammable materials which must be stored in dry
and airy places, away from heat sources and open flames,
stacked on shelves or in drawers.

Veneer is a sheet material that is made from various types
of wood (thin slices of oak, ash, walnut, teak, balsa, etc.).
Other wood sheet materials used by model builders are plywood (layers of veneer bonded so that the grain of each ply
or layer runs at 90 degrees to that of the adjacent layers)
and various kinds of hardboard made from wood pulp such
as MDF, chipboard, etc. The thickness of these wood–based
sheet materials ranges from one millimetre (veneer) to several centimetres (chipboard) (Fig. 4.26). A range of tools are
used to cut them, from hand cutters to circular saws to jigsaws, depending on the thickness of the material and other cutting requirements. Like paper, wood is a highly flammable material and must be stored in dry and ventilated
places, away from open flame and heat sources. Veneer is
stored on horizontal shelves (it is often kept in rolls), while
other, thicker materials may be kept vertically.

Cork is a lightweight natural material, which is produced
and sold in the form of thin sheets of different dimensions
and thicknesses. Similar to paperboard, it is cut with laser
cutters or sharp cutting tools such as scalpels or knives.

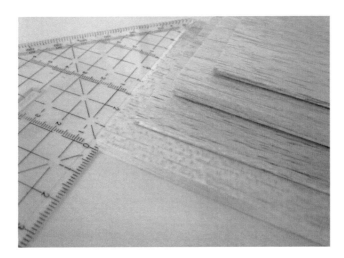

Fig. 4.26 *Balsa sheets of various types and thicknesses*

Styrofoam (closed–cell extruded polystyrene foam) is a lightweight material produced and sold as sheets of various thicknesses. This category of materials includes Styrofoam sheets which are not thicker than 4 centimetres. Styrofoam is cut with scalpels and knives, as well as hot–wire foam cutters. It falls in the group of materials which melt when exposed to heat and emit poisonous gases. This is why it should be stored in dry and ventilated places, away from open flames and heat sources, on horizontal shelves or in upright racks.

Plastic is a material which is most frequently used in the form of foil or sheets of different dimensions. It is often coloured, and it may also be transparent or opaque, as well as glossy or matte. It is manufactured in the form of solid sheets (acrylic glass, PVC, polystyrene, etc.); also, it may consist of two or more ingredients (e.g., Lexan). Plastic also comes in the form of plastic netting or meshes produced in a range of colours and of varying density (Fig. 4.27).

Different cutting tools are used with different types of plastic (knives or scalpels, scribers, saws, etc.). Unlike cell–cast acrylic glass (Plexiglas), extruded acrylic glass can be easily cut with laser cutters. It is produced and sold as colourless or coloured, in sheets of different thicknesses and degrees of transparency. Depending on the thickness of the acrylic sheet, the obtained cut may be slightly conical in shape due to the melting of the material and the beam divergence. It is recommended to cut acrylic glass with the protective foil on to avoid the effects described above.

Manipulating and working with acrylic glass may leave traces on the surface of the material, which are removed using a soft cloth and a mild cleanser. Otherwise, the face of the sheet may become "foggy" or "cloudy". Plastic is also a highly flammable and poisonous material, which is why all types are not cut with a laser and must also be kept at a safe distance from heat sources and open flames. When planning to use a laser cutter with plastic, one should check with the salesperson prior to the purchase to know which particular plastic material can be laser–cut. Depending on how thick they are, plastic materials are stored in rolls, stacked on shelves or in drawers, or kept in upright racks.

Fig. 4.27 *Various plastic materials*

Glass is used in scale modelling only in special cases, i.e., when there are special requirements for its application. Model builders use glass sheets of various sizes and thicknesses (minimum 2 mm). Glass is a highly fragile material and must be handled with extreme caution. It is cut with diamond knives or water jet cutters and finished with special tools. It should always be stored in upright racks protected against impact.

Sheet metal (e.g., galvanised tin, copper, aluminium, and less commonly steel or stainless steel) is only rarely used in scale modelling. It is sold in sheets of various sizes and properties, and in case there are special requirements, metal meshes are also available. A range of special tools are used for cutting and processing sheet metal (shears, cutting knives, etc.), including CNC milling machines. Sheet metal is stored in dry places and away from moisture to prevent corrosion. Thin sheet metal is often kept in rolls, while thicker and heavier sheets are stored on shelves, or less frequently in upright racks.

4.3.2   Linear Materials

A material whose diametre (R) or depth–to–thickness ratio (b:c) is negligible compared to its length (a) is called a linear material. These materials are most often wood, plastic or metal. The cross–section of linear materials, usually in the form of battens, bars and strips, may be angular (square, b:b, or rectangular, b:c) or circular (R). Battens/bars are kept in dry and ventilated places, in open boxes, in which they are sorted according to material and size. Strip materials, when in rolls, are kept either on shelves or in drawers. Battens/bars are used for manufacturing rigid workpieces, usually structural members like columns and beams (stick construction), components of spherical structures (geodesic dome or free–form geodesic structures), as well as components of cylindrical and conical structures, hyperbolic paraboloids, etc.

Wood strips are the type of strips most commonly used in scale modelling. They come in different cross–sections and lengths and are made of different kinds of wood (Fig. 4.28). They may be cut with mini or hobby wood saws. Plastic strips are made of cast, pressed or extruded hard plastic. Nylon fibre of different diametres in coils is also used. Plastic strips are cut with scissors and special knives, as well as plastic–cutting saws. Like wood strips, they should be kept away from open flame and heat sources, and coils should be stored on shelves or in drawers.

Metal rods/bars or wire are mainly solid, not pipes, and come in various diametres, which generally do not exceed Ø 0.30. Metal bars and wire are cut with cutting pliers/pincers, shears and metal–cutting saws. Metal–polishing sandpaper is used for smoothening the ends of the cut pieces. Bars are kept either laid on shelves or stored vertically in open wooden boxes. Wire coils are kept on shelves or in drawers.

Fig. 4.28 *Wood dowels, strips and battens*

4.3.3 Volumetric Materials

Materials which are manufactured in approximately regular or equilateral shapes, i.e., which are of the same or approximately the same length (a), width (b) and height (c), are known as volumetric materials. This group also comprises cylindrically–shaped materials, whose diametre (R) is in due proportion to its height (c). Wood is one of the most commonly used volumetric materials, but metal and plastic are used just as frequently. Generally, these materials are cut with milling machines and lathes, including the latest CNC milling centres.

Wood is the most widely and commonly used volumetric modelling material. Special kinds of wood such as rose, box-wood, walnut, etc., as well as exotic wood like teak, ebony, balsa, etc., are generally used to produce either individual components or entire models. They may be cut/processed with lathes and wood milling machines, as well as manually with wood–carving tools. Only completely dry timber should be used in scale modelling to avoid the danger of the subsequent deformation of the components. Dry timber is stored on shelves; where necessary and possible, the store-room should be continuously ventilated with dry air.

Styrofoam and other polystyrene materials are lightweight materials which are manufactured and sold in blocks of different sizes and thicknesses. These materials are cut with scalpels, knives and hot–wire foam cutters. There are many kinds of materials made from polystyrene, differing in cell size and uniformity, texture consistency and colour (Fig. 4.29). EPS (expanded polystyrene) and XPS (extruded polystyrene foam) are sold in different colours, with the physical properties of individual products varying significantly. Before cutting the material, it is recommended to check the size of the component(s) by cutting a sample with the selected tool and to adjust the cutter settings accordingly. Styrofoam may be cut with pieces of wire of different diametres. To obtain non–standard forms, it is cut with CNC milling machines and then impregnated with special substances. This method is commonly used by model makers to build ground models.

Fig. 4.29 *Various types
of Styrofoam/polystyrene
materials*

4.3.4 Materials Used to Model Amorphous Shapes

Building a scale model may require modelling amorphous shapes, for which materials other than those mentioned or discussed previously in the text are used. They may be earth, clay, modelling clay/plasticine, sponge, textile, various kinds of nets and meshes, straw, rubber strips, or any other material available to the model builder. The differences between these materials and their distinctive characteristics make them suitable for the manufacturing of various types of models, from conceptual to final, including very complex geometric shapes, such as free–form and tent–like structures (stretching structures).

The cutting and processing methods used with these materials depend on the characteristics of each individual material, how and what it will be used for, and the shape of the scale model that will be built from it. The upkeep of these materials also depends on their distinctive properties. For instance, earth is kept in sacks, clay in airtight/vacuum sealer bags, and others may be kept in boxes, bales, etc. As there are many types of clay which vary in grain fineness and colour, ranging from terracotta to brown, one should be familiar with these different properties before opting for a specific type. Clay is used in manual scale modelling (Fig. 4.30) and the quality or fineness of the model depends on the model builder's skills.

Fig. 4.30 *Various tools are used when modelling clay by hand, Smart Geometry Workshop 2012*

The latest trend in clay modelling is cutting clay to CAD–generated shapes with thin wire stretched in a frame controlled via a robot arm (Fig. 4.31).

Fig. 4.31 *Clay shapes cut with a robot arm, Smart Geometry Workshop 2012*

4.3.5 Smart Materials

Smart materials are those materials whose properties change, mostly under external influences. External influences are those exerted by the material surroundings, such as light, heat or touch. They may affect the mechanical and electrical properties of smart materials, as well as their physical qualities, such as structure and composition, which often also influences their function. According to Addington and Schodek [1], depending on the type of change caused in these materials by environmental factors (chemical, mechanical, electrical, magnetic or thermal), they may be classified as:

—   Thermochromic – an input of thermal energy (heat) to the material alters its molecular structure, leading to colour change.

—   Magnetorheological and electrorheological – the application of a magnetic field or an electrical field causes a change in micro–structural orientation, resulting in a change in the viscosity of a fluid.

—   Thermotropic, phototropic, electrotropic – an input of energy (thermal energy for thermotropic, radiation for phototropic, electricity for electrotropic, and so on) to the material alters its micro–structure through a phase change. Most materials demonstrate different properties in different phases, which may include conductivity, transmissivity, volumetric expansion, and solubility.

—   Shape memory – an input of thermal energy (which can also be produced through resistance to an electrical current) alters the micro–structure through a crystalline phase change. This change enables multiple shapes in relationship to the environmental stimulus.

Due to these these properties, smart materials are also called responsive materials or functional materials. There are many different smart material categories, some of which may be of particular interest for use in scale modelling, such as colour–changing materials, light–emitting materials and self–assembling materials.

Fig. 4.32 HygroScope - Meteorosensitive Morphology, Achim Menges in collaboration with Steffen Reichert, Centre Pompidou, Paris, 2012

Apart from these, there are also self–diagnostic materials, temperature–changing materials (Fig. 4.32, Fig. 4.33, Fig. 4.34), moving materials, and many others. There has been a growing interest in new materials, not only in lab research but also for application purposes. In the last few years, there has been experimental research into the use of smart materials in architecture. In the SmartScreen project by the Decker Yeadon architectural studio thermal sensitive materials were used to build a solar shading system opening and closing in response to the changing room temperature [3]. It allowed continuous regulation of heat transfer without using a HVAC system or consuming electric power.

Fig. 4.33 HygroScope project: closed structure as a response to relative humidity within its microenvironment of the glass case

Fig. 4.34 According to the project description, when the humidity level rises, the system changes its surface porosity to breathe and ventilate the moisture saturated air; the climate changes within the case directly influence the systems behaviour

Another approach is used in the Phototropia project carried out in the Master of Advanced Studies class at the Chair for CAAD at ETH Zurichin 2012 and supervised by Manuel Kretzer. Smart materials (electro–active polymers and electro–luminescent displays)were used to build a conceptual architectural model that uses solar energy and responds to user presence through moving and illuminating elements [8].

Smart materials are most often used in cases where the changes they undergo are carefully planned for improved performance, i.e., for the purpose of improving specific, often predefined uses or qualities (Fig. 4.35, Fig. 4.36). They are likely to be increasingly used in a range of fields, including architectural scale modelling.

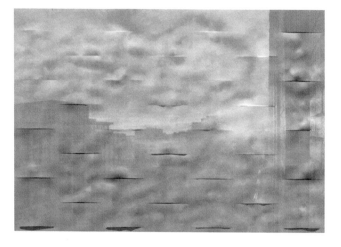

Fig. 4.35 Decker Yeadon LLC, Smart Screen project, version one: a solar shading system opening and closing in response to the changing room temperature

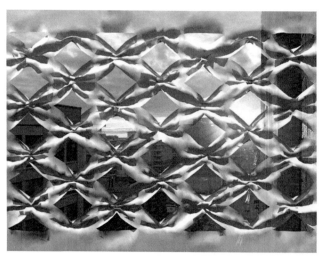

Fig. 4.36 Smart Screen project, version one: changed shape of screen as a response to a regulation of heat transfer

Also very important are traditional materials found in nature that behave like engineered, man–made smart materials, which are not the product of new technologies. The research design project HygroScope – Meteorosensitive Morphology, carried out by the design team comprising Prof. Achim Menges, Steffen Reichert, and Boyan Mihaylov at the Institute for Computational Design (ICD) in Stuttgart, studied the responsive capacities of wood, based on its hygroscopic behaviour and anisotropic characteristics. It came after the Responsive Surface Structures project by Steffen Reichert, conducted as part of Menges' course Form Generation and Materialisation at the Hochschule für Gestaltung Offenbach, Germany [4], and followed more than five years of research into climatic responsive architectural systems that do not require any sensory equipment or motor functions [7]. According to the project description, the HygroScope – Meteorosensitive Morphology project features a wooden model suspended within a glass case with controlled humidity. Changes to the level of humidity in the glass case directly impact the shape of the model. The project shows that wood veneer can be used as a responsive material, capable of changing shape in accordance with influences of the environment; it is also possible to use wood as a smart material for building planar structures/surfaces whose porosity alters relative to external humidity. The key parameters observed in these projects, such as the grain direction and the width, length and thickness of the veneer, may affect the way in which a structure behaves in response to relative humidity in the surroundings [4].

4.3.6   Additional Materials

The term "additional materials" refers to factory–made prefabricated or ready–to–assemble model components or items. These materials are normally sold in specialised model or hobby shops and added in the final stage of model building, usually as decoration. They include a broad range of products such as moss, grass, trees, human figures, automobiles, ships, airplanes, railway objects (rails, train stations, tunnels, engines, cars and switches), etc. These components and items are mass–produced in a range of designs and sizes. They are often made of putty to be used as components that are subsequently installed in the model and painted as necessary. Also, they may be purchased as completed preassembled items. These additional materials are used to represent an array of objects and elements used by model builders to make their replicas true–to–life. When it comes to architectural scale modelling, human figures are by all means the most frequently used ready–made items. They come in various sizes to be used with models built to different standard scales, which they "scale up" to human size. Human figures are sold monochrome and painted according to need.

The additional materials used in architectural scale modelling also include various lighting items and equipment. To show the structure and details of the original building as clearly and effectively as possible, the scale model is often lit with additional lighting, most frequently from the inside, and less often from the outside. The basic items or gear needed to "wire" the scale model are diodes, switches, batteries or an adaptor, and wire; quite often, a potentiometre is also needed. The additional materials come in a range of packaging, and the number of items sold in individual packs also varies. These materials are stored in drawers or small boxes, with partitions used to sort materials and figures according to properties and size ratio for easier storage and handling.

4.4   Colour

Architectural scale builders use colour in different ways. Monochrome scale models that are the original colour of the material used (wood, plastic, metal or glass) are both the neatest and the most appealing. Monochrome scale models allow the viewer to see and learn as much as possible about the structure, shape and details of the building represented by the replica (see Fig. 3.7, Chapter 3). Excessive use of colour may distract the viewer and turn attention away from elements or parts which are important to the choice of colour, which is not as relevant. Building a scale model often requires combining different materials, and it is absolutely necessary to stop the colour of any individual material from stealing the show. In such cases, painting the entire model is a better solution. It is best to paint the scale model one colour with a spray gun with an adjustable nozzle, which ensures even the smallest pieces of the model are painted thoroughly and with precision. Aerosol paint may be used with small–size scale models, but applying it with precision and in a quality manner requires some experience and ex-

treme caution. Brushes are not frequently used for monochrome painting. This subject was dealt with previously in
this chapter, in the painting tool descriptions.

Realistic scale models, like those respresenting structures
or buildings listed as national or historical landmarks must
be true representations of the originals, i.e., the materials
and colours used to build a model should be as close to the
original as possible (see Fig. 3.14, Chapter 3). Scale models
of this type are painted by hand with brushes of different
kinds and sizes. The paint used on scale models is typically
water–based (acrylic paint), because it dries fast and causes
minimum pollution in the working space.

Along with the types of paint traditionally used in scale
modelling, which may be purchased in specialised model
or arts and crafts shops, it is likely that "smart" or "intelligent" substances will be used in near future. There are
materials which change colour, which may be classified as
photochromic and thermochromic. Photochromic materials
change colour temporarily relative to the intensity of the
light they receive. When in a dark room, these materials are
usually colorless, but when struck by sunlight or ultraviolet
light, their molecular structure alters and starts reflecting
colour. Colour vanishes with the removal of the light source.
Colour change may be "designed" or "programmed" by
mixing photochromic and ordinary paint, thus influencing
which hue will be reflected when the mixture is exposed
to a source of light. The effects achieved by using "smart"
paint may be combined with those of the model lighting,
by making selected parts of the scale model reflect specific
colours when the lighting is turned on. Thermochromic materials change colour reversibly with the changing temperature of the surroundings. They are either semiconductor
liquid crystals or metal compounds. Their colour changes
at specified temperatures, which may vary depending on
the thickness of the applied material. Because they possess
such characteristics, it is necessary to plan the model presentation carefully and concurrently with the model building.
Thermochromic materials may be used to good advantage
in performance–based design and on facades which change
colour based on the energy received through insolation.
The appearance of different colours or different shades of
one colour on the facade of a building can be effected by
the fluctuating light intensity or thermal energy absorbed
by the facade. In any case, these new "smart" materials will

most certainly change the underlying principles of analogue scale modelling. We believe they will soon be used extensively in digital and automated scale modelling, either as components or by affecting at least one of the modelling stages.

In the next chapter we discuss the procedures and methods of preparation, as well as the realisation of the various elements a scale models consists of. The realised parts or elements must be carefully joined together to make the completed model, which is then finished with the aim of being representative of the replicated building and so fulfil its purpose.

References

[1]   Addington,M., Schodek, D.: Smart Materials And New Technologies: For the Architecture and Design Professions, Architectural Press (2004)

[2]   Dunn, N.: Come realizzare un modelo architettonico. Logos, Modena (2010)

[3]   Decker Yeadon LLC, Project Smart Screen I, II, III. http://www.deckeryeadon.com/projects.html Accessed 3 Dec 2012

[4]   Hensel, M., Menges, A., Sunguroğlu, D.: Material Performance. Architectural Design. 78(2), 34–41 (2008)

[5]   Knoll, W., Hechinger, M.: Architektur – Modelle Anregungen zu ihrem Bau. Deutsche Verlags –Anstalt, München (2006)

[6]   Mills B. C.: Designing with models – A Studio Guide to Making and Using Architectural Design Models. John Wiley & Sons, Inc. Hoboken, New Jersey (2005)

[7]   Menges A., Reichert, S.: HygroScope – Meteorosensitive Morphology. Project description Centre Pompidou Paris (2012)

[8]   Responsive Design blog http://responsivedesignstudio.blogspot.com/2012/05/phototropia.html Accessed 3 Dec 2012

[9]   Šiđanin, P., Tepavčević, B.: Maketarstvo za studente arhitekture. FTN, Novi Sad (2010)

5 MANUFACTURING SCALE MODELS & SCALE MODEL COMPONENTS: METHODS AND PROCESSES

5 MANUFACTURING SCALE MODELS & SCALE MODEL COMPONENTS: METHODS AND PROCESSES

The geometric structures used in architectural design nowadays are far more complex than those before digital techniques were introduced. Consequently, an architect using elements of complex geometry in his or her designs has to have good knowledge of manufacturing methods which make design realisation possible. Making scale models for the needs of such designs is a key step in the process of design development; it is an early stage of the process during which structural connections may be tested in a physical environment during assembly, allowing the preclusion of any problems or deficiencies that may arise later in the process.

This chapter discusses the possibilities of digital scale modelling that allow for greater precision and efficiency, as well as the technical and practical skills needed to make scale models. It also gives instructions on how to display, transport, light and photograph the finished scale model to create quality records of the model, which may be included in the design/project documentation.

Making scale models in the digital age requires much more than mere manual skills. One should be familar with digital fabrication techniques, their comparative advantages and deficiencies, as well as with digital modelling and fabrication software. The introduction of digital methods to modelling may be linked to the increasing complexity of architectural designs and of their scale modelling. This is essential because these shapes consist of non–standardised components. Most often, they are prototypes whose structural integrity and other properties are tested using analogue models, to confirm their soundness for construction purposes.

Along with the necessary technical knowledge, building scale models requires a lot of patience, precision and orderliness. The making of any model (with the exception of conceptual and interim models) passes through a number of predefined development phases meant to ensure the efficiency of the process and the quality required of the produced model. These are the main steps in the scale modelling process:

— studying the design,
— making digital 2D drawings in preparaton for cutting,
— material cutting and final processing /defect repair,
— gluing the components,
— assembling the model, and
— finishing the model.

Each of these phases of scale modelling is divided into subphases and contains additional steps. These subphases and steps depend on the techniques and materials used to realise a model, as well as the complexity of the object or building it should represent. For instance, when modelling double curved surfaces, it is essential to select an optimal manufacturing method in relation to the building shape of the object. 3D printers may be used in such cases, but a virtual model must first be generated using CAD software and exported in the right format. Next, it may be laser–cut out of a two–dimensional or sheet material.

To prepare the components needed for the scale model, the geometry of the object is simplified by its discretisation into segments and their flattening on a two–dimensional plane. These two fabrication methods require quite different CAD approaches to modelling or drawing two–dimensional components. Obviously, manufacturing the scale model of an object whose geometry is complex is considerably more complicated than that of an object consisting of planar elements, since it requires a greater amount of technical effort and time to prepare the components for fabrication.

During the first phase of the scale model realisation process, the design is studied in order to adopt the most effective and purposeful fabrication procedure, which largely depends on the underlying concept of the design. In this respect, the fabrication must be carried out in such a way as to ensure the guiding principle of the concept is easily identifiable in the completed scale model (transparency of the object, lightness, solidity vs. voidness, etc.).

5.1   Architectural Design Study

When studying an architectural design for the purpose of scale modelling, there are three different types of analysis:

- final design study,
- design study through interim scale model analysis, and
- conceptual design study.

Final design study refers to the analysis of working drawings, based on which a scale model is made for the purpose of representing the given object or building.

Studying the design through interim scale model analysis means the scale model may play a part in the design development process. This type of study entails trying different modelling techniques, experimenting with different materials or finding an original way of making or styling a scale model.

Conceptual design study refers to the analysis of the designed shapes and attempts to transform ideas into three-dimensional physical models.

5.1.1   Final design study

When the realisation of a scale model requires the participation of a person who has not been directly involved in the design development, a meticulous analysis of the design is necessary for this person to understand it as well as possible. This analysis involves the examination of the technical documentation and drawings, as well as all the existing interim scale models.

The first step in making a scale model is a detailed study of the design elements, preliminary or final. The immediate surroundings of the object or building should be examined first when beginning to analyse the design. This is done by analysing the site plan with the intention of observing and taking into account all elements that might help when placing the scale model into the surroundings. This is followed by a detailed examination of the general arrangement drawings, cross–sections, elevations and details of the design. If a virtual 3D model is available, it should also be studied. The purpose of this analysis is to understand the physical or spatial arrangement of the elements and the structural system used, which is decisive in selecting the manufacturing procedure. It is necessary to agree with the client on how detailed the scale model should be and on the approximate budget for the final scale model at this stage.

These input parameters will help select the fabrication technique (laser cutting, different types of 3D printing, 3D milling, etc.). Only then should a plan be conceived that covers the components to be made first, what type of base the scale model will be placed on, the building frame, load–bearing walls, skin, etc. This may also influence the choice of materials for the scale model. After these important decisions have been made, one may proceed with disassembling the 3D model, drawing 2D elements, specifying the types of connections between the members, establishing the procedure for assembling the components, etc.

When it comes to final designs, digital models will already have been made for the purpose of 2D visualisation (ground plans, cross–sections, elevations), or 3D models will have been completed for 3D presentation (rendering) in most cases. Many of these models cannot be used as scale models in their existing form. They usually contain too much information, which needs to be reduced in accordance with the amount of detail and complexity required for the scale model. Some other models may call for additional details or information for the purpose of 3D visualisation. How to modify the digital model for the purposes of scale modelling by omitting extra information or adding new elements is explained in greater detail further below.

5.1.2   Terrain modelling

A scale model does not simply represent an object, but also the terrain which the object is located on. The modelling technique used may vary depending on the scale of the model and the size of the terrain. The model may be realistic and correspond to the actual site, or it may be abstract,

with the object placed in an arbitrary setting bearing no relation to the site.

Realistic terrain models show all the existing natural and
man–made features of the terrain or site. These models
may take the following forms:

–   two–dimensional lines showing the plot boundaries, ac-
    cess roads and walkways, and the objects found on the
    plot, or

–   3D terrain models showing ground elevations/levels,
    with three–dimensional replicas of both the natural
    enivronment and man–made objects (e.g., with the
    vegetation made distinct from the rest of the environ-
    ment/objects).

Abstract terrain models, arbitrarily showing the area surrounding an object, may contain man–made objects and
street furniture to establish a sense of the scale and size of
the model.

Thinking about the purpose of the scale model should help
to select between one of the two types of terrain models.
Making the right selection is important for any subsequent
work on the model of the object, as well as choosing the
right manufacturing method, materials and scale. For example, very steep ground will inevitably play a crucial role in
the design of the building to be constructed on it; accordingly, the scale model should also represent and be made
taking such terrain into account.

A contour map and a plan showing all the access roads and
walkways (with the cuts and fills) are needed to make the
terrain model of a site. Very often, the only data available
are the elevations across the broader surroundings of the
object. In such cases the terrain must be surveyed and the
collected data is then used to produce a smooth three–dimensional terrain model. Fig. 5.1 shows a terrain model
generated as a NURBS surface.

In the first step horizontal sections of the ground must be
made to create the contours to represent a surface. The
depth of the horizontal sections will vary depending on the
material selected for the terrain model.

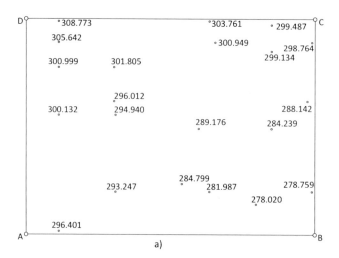

a)

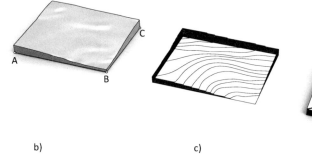

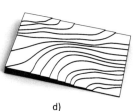

b)   c)   d)

Fig. 5.1 Elevations (a) are used to generate the NURBS surface (b), the contours (c) needed to produce a terrain model (d)

If a volumetric material is cut with a CNC milling machine to create a scale model, the section depths will depend on the amount and complexity of the available field data, with the milling machine cutting along the contours. The depths of the sections made out of two–dimensional materials (e.g., cardboard) used to make the scale model will be relative to the material thickness.

Next, the contours may be extruded using a 3D virtual terrain model to obtain the equidistances (the height differences between the adjacent contours), with the resulting virtual model corresponding to the analogue terrain model. The contours are arranged on the sheets of the material to be laser cut before being cut out as two–dimensional elements (Fig. 5.2). Before this is done, proper consideration must be given to how the model will be put together, some additional steps and procedures might help make this easier.

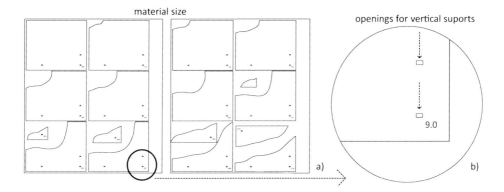

material size

openings for vertical suports

9.0

a)

b)

For instance, the components ought to be designated with marks that can be engraved on the material. This may be done in a number of ways, depending on the complexity of the model, and the marks could be numbers, letters or combinations of symbols clearly indicating the position of each component and its adjoining parts. Whenever possible, the marks should be made in places that will not be visible on the completed scale model. It is easiest to fix the cut components with vertical struts as they are set in their positions, one on top of the other to ensure the greatest precision.

To achieve greater structural stability, it is advisable to use a minimum of three vertical supports. The openings for these vertical supports should be made in the material just below the uppermost section or layer, so they stay hidden after the components have been glued. After the sections have been cut out, they are stacked one on top of another and glued together. The vertical supports used to facilitate stacking also increases the structural stability of the model. Fig. 5.3 shows the various steps of the building process and the completed terrain model.

In large models, it is often necessary to divide the horizontal sections into smaller parts before cutting them out. In such cases, one must make sure the part connections are not placed immediately one above another as this might affect the stability of the model. These models require large quantities of material so one must always keep optimal material use in mind. Only strips wide enough to ensure the stability of the model should be cut out to make the most efficient use of the material, not complete sections (Fig. 5.4).

Fig. 5.2 Component arrangement for laser cutting (a) with a number–designated component (b)

Fig. 5.3 Building a terrain model

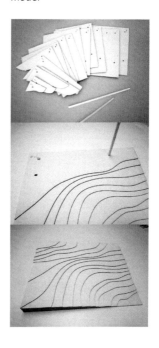

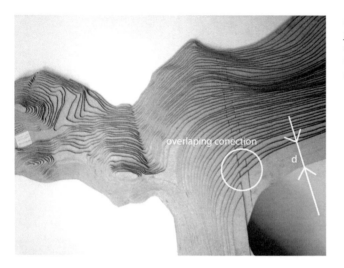

Fig. 5.4 Large hollow models for the optimal use of material, with overlapping connections to avoid destabilising the model

5.1.3   Geometric shape analysis

Geometric shape analysis refers to the identification of geometric shapes in architectural design elements. In terms of the geometry of objects or buildings, the basic distinction made is between planar and curved structures. Those components which consist of planar elements may be made from standardised materials. The cutting preparations for these elements are examined in the next chapter.

Many contemporary designs feature curved elements, which makes them hard to replicate using traditional scale modelling methods and materials. Geometric analysis, that addresses the issues of size, shape, the relative position of a shape in a complex figure and its characteristics in relation to physical space, is needed to model such elements.

Curved surfaces are classified in many different ways, depending on the field or discipline in which they are discussed [1],[2],[3],[4],[5]. In general, there are several classifications of curved surfaces in geometry, which are differentiated by how they are generated or by their properties. Some of those types of surfaces are of particular interest for architectural design, such as ruled surfaces (hyperbolic paraboloids, conoids, helicoids, one–sheet rotational hyperboloid, etc.), arbitrary surfaces (NURBS surfaces, Bézier surfaces, etc.), minimal surfaces (catenoids, gyroids, Catalan's surfaces, etc.), and non–orientable surfaces (Klein bottles, Möbius strips, etc.). No matter which surface is selected for scale modelling, one must understand it and be familiar with its geometric characteristics.

A property which bears great relevance for scale modelling is surface curvature (Fig. 5.5). For analysing surface curvature we can use tangent planes. A tangent plane touches a surface in a point P. If all tangent planes touch a curved surface along lines m the surface is single curved (Fig. 5.5a). If a tangent plane touches a surface only in one point P and the surface lies on one side of the tangent plane the surface has positive curvature in P (Fig. 5.5b). If the tangent plane intersects the surface in P it has a negative curvature in P.

The simplest examples of single curved surfaces are the cylinder and the cone. Single curved surfaces are also known as developable surfaces, as they may be flattened out onto a plane. This property of single curved surfaces is very important because it allows creating patterns which may be cut out of a planar material and then bent, rolled or folded to achieve the desired shape. Single curved surfaces are most easily flattened out using the digital tools offered by software packages such as Rhinoceros, Autodesk Inventor or Catia. These surfaces are also ruled surfaces. They can be generated by moving a straight line.

They are particularly important for contemporary architectural practice, more precisely, for scale modelling, because components shaped as developable surfaces may be made using single sheets of paper, veneer or other flexible materials, without any stretching or cutting.

Fig. 5.5 *Surface curvature*

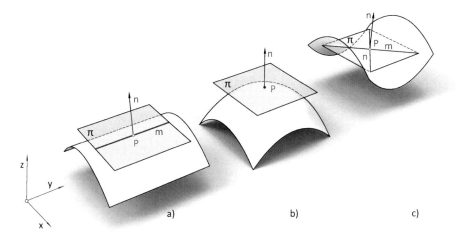

a)   b)   c)

When it comes to geometrically complex architectural designs, complex surfaces are often discretised into singly curved elements to optimise construction costs.

The simplest example of a double curved surface with positive curvature is the sphere, and that of a double curved surface with negative curvature the hyperbolic paraboloid. Double curved surfaces cannot be flattened out. To develop this type of surface into a flat mesh, its geometry must be altered. To do this, double curved surfaces are simplified (discretised) into segments of single curved surfaces (developable surface) or planar elements. Examples of these two types of discretisation and mesh development are shown in Fig. 5.6 and Fig. 5.7.

When it comes to double curved surfaces, it is necessary to identify the geometric shape of the object first and then accordingly select a production method for the model components to be assembled later. In architecture, the most commonly used double curved surfaces (in the traditional sense) are the sphere, hyperbolic paraboloid and one–sheet rotational hyperboloid. The following examples illustrate the discretisation of two double curved surfaces, one with positive and one with negative curvature. The term discretisation refers to the division of a surface into segments to simplify its structure, increase its stability and facilitate construction. Depending on the specific requirements, the materials used and the realisation procedure, a surface may be discretised into singly curved elements or planar elements.

Fig. 5.6 Discretisation into cylindrical segments

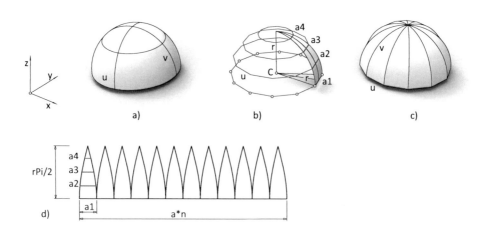

a)   b)   c)

d)

By studying the intrinsic geometry of the sphere (Fig. 5.6a), it may be concluded that it consists of two sets of curves respectively marked with letters u and v. The u–direction curves are circles and the v–direction curves are quarter–circles. The u–direction curves are discretised to discretise the entire sphere into cylindrical segments. The u–direction curves may be converted into a series of lines, i.e. each circle may be poligonised to form the desired number of hemispherical segments. In terms of geometry, a second–order curve (circle) is converted into first–order curves (polyline) by discretisation. In our case u–circles are incircles of regular polygons.

There is no need to discretise the v–direction curves. The u–direction polylines and the v–direction curves are used to construct cylindrical surfaces of the sphere segments (Fig. 5.6b). All generatrices of these cylindrical surfaces are parts of the discretized u–curves. Fig. 5.6c shows the discretised sphere consisting of twelve hemishperical segments. To develop the sphere into a mesh (see Fig. 5.6c), one of the segments is first flattened and then multiplied by the number of segments the dome consists of. To build the mesh, the actual lengths of the quarter–circle and of the cylindrical surface generator lines (a1, a2, a3 and a4) are calculated. The easiest way to construct the border curves is by interpolating a curve through the end points of a1, a2, a3 and a4 generatrices. In fact the spatial border curves are parts of ellipses and the flattened versions are parts of sinus curves.

Another possibility to model a double curved surface is to discretise it into a triangular mesh and to flatten it. Basically, a surface can be arbitrarily covered with a number of points which can be connected by triangles. This triangle mesh is a first rough approximation of the surface. To improve the approximation the triangles can be divided into smaller triangles with new vertices on it. These vertices are then projected onto the original double curved surface. There they form new triangles which are used further.

Fig. 5.7 shows the discretisation of the sphere by a Platonic solid – icosahedron. First, a icosahedron is inscribed inside the sphere and each of its faces is divided into triangles. The vertices of the triangles are projected in the direction of their normals out of the centre of the sphere to the curved surface, creating a new polyhedron – the first stage of discretisation.

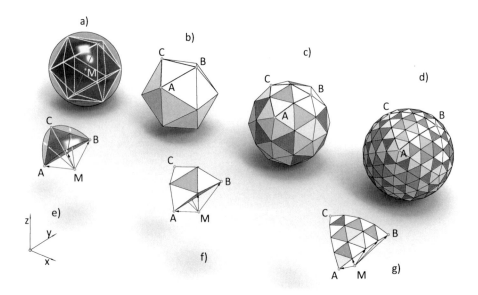

Depending on the desired size of the elements, this procedure may be repeated several times. The advantage of descretizing the sphere by a Platonic solid is that in the first stage only two triangle shapes and in the second stage only four different shapes are generated. The shown procedure can also be accomplished by Archemedean solids, but it yields more different shapes. Fig. 5.8 shows the mesh of the discretised spheres shown in Fig. 5.7.

Fig. 5.7 *Discretisation of the sphere into planar elements*

Fig. 5.8 *a) Flattened mesh of the discretised sphere of Fig. 5.7c, b) Flattened mesh of the discretised sphere of Fig. 5.7d*

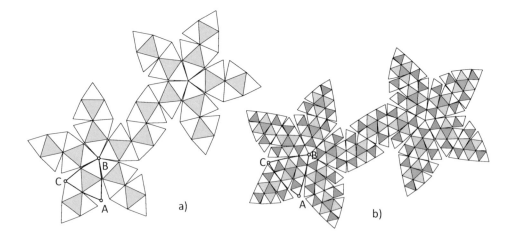

The hyperbolic paraboloid and the one–sheet rotational hyperboloid are negative double curved surfaces. The one–sheet rotational hyperboloid (Fig. 5.9c) can be generated by revolving one part of a hyperbola h around the minor axis a (Fig. 5.9a, Fig. 5.9e). The one–sheet rotational hyperboloid can be also generated as a ruled surface. It is generated by revolving a skew line m around an axis a (Fig. 5.9b, Fig.5.9d). This characteristic makes this surfaces immediately applicable in the construction industry. This shape is commonly used in the design of buildings such as water and cooling towers, and its elements are easily recognisable in contemporary architectural designs.

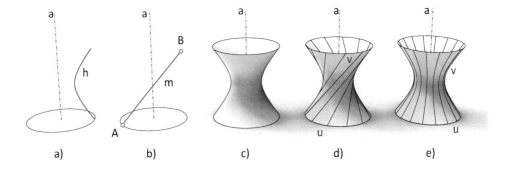

a) b) c) d) e)

Making scale models of one–sheet rotational hyperboloids whose structure consist of lines is possible by using bars that have the position of v lines shown in Fig. 5.9d. The one–sheet rotational hyperboloid consists of two line systems (Fig. 5.10a and Fig. 5.10b) that give additional stability to the whole structure (Fig. 5.10c). The second possibility to build such hyperboloid models is to discretise them into developable surfaces as explained in Fig. 5.6.

Fig. 5.9 The one–sheet rotational hyperboloid –different kind of generation

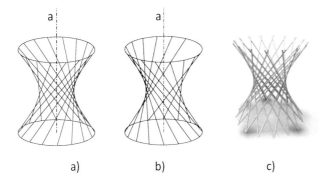

a) b) c)

Fig. 5.10 The one–sheet rotational hyperboloid – two line systems

In this case the *u*–direction curves which are actually circles (Fig. 5.9e) will be descretised into regular polygons and furthermore, the surface will be discretised into cylindrical segments that can be developed into a flattened mesh.

The hyperbolic paraboloid – HP (Fig. 5.11) is a ruled surface that consists of two systems of skew lines. All lines in one system lie on parallel planes. If we take a skew rectangle ABCD and divide its edges AB and CD into equal segments and connect them, we get the first line system (Fig. 5.11a). For the second system we have to divide the edges BC and DA in the same way as before. If we do this in an infinite way, we get a smooth surface as shown in Fig. 5.11b. The Fig. 5.11c shows the extended HP with parabolas *p* as border curves.

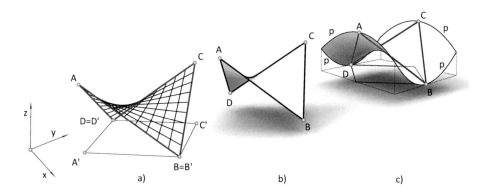

a)   b)   c)

A simple method for making scale models in the form of the HP (hyper shells) is by using four support bars correspond to the inclinations of the first and last generators lines like the skew quadrangle ABCD in 5.11a. Thereafter strips of material (paper or thin paperboard, veneer, plastic foil, or thin balsa) are placed one next to another to achieve the desired shape.

Fig. 5.11 Hyperbolic paraboloid as a ruled surface discretised into a mesh

Apart from the procedure described above, there are other interesting ways to model hyperbolic paraboloids (Fig. 5.12). The hyperbolic paraboloid is a translational surface that is generated by moving a parabola *p* along another parabola *q* serving as the directrix. Both parabolas must have parallel axes (*a1, a2*) and have to be open on different sides.

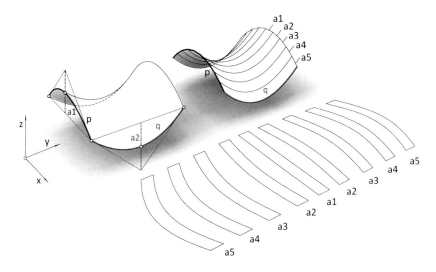

The hyperbolic paraboloid may be discretised into single curved surfaces, i.e. parabolic cylinders. They can be developed in order to flatten the hyperbolic paraboloid into a mesh. In Fig. 5.12 the parabola p is discretised into a polyline that consists of nine lines. Through every vertex of the polyline, we take on of the parallel parabolas q.

A parabolic cylinder can be generated between two adjacent parabolas. Therefore, the HP can be discretised into a flat mesh consisting of nine cylindrical surfaces. In terms of of symmetric reason, we have only stripes of five different shapes.

Apart from the shapes discussed above, other ruled surfaces are often found in architecture, such as Catalan's surfaces, conoids, and helicoids (Fig. 5.13).

Fig. 5.12 *Reparametrisation of the hyperbolic paraboloid and the resulting mesh*

Fig. 5.13 *Helicoid and aproximation of the mesh*

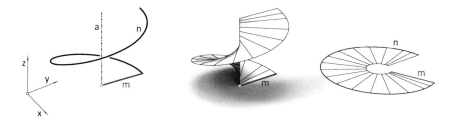

Catalan's surfaces and helicoids are often used in scale modelling to make spiral stairs. The fact that ruled surfaces are generated by moving a straight line to its different positions makes it possible to used them in scale modelling. Similar to the hyperbolic paraboloids, it is often sufficent to manufacture some "bearing members", which are deduced from the u– or v–lines of the surfaces, like the border curves, for instance. Then strips made from a thin flexible material can be placed between the members. If the surfaces are slightly curved, it is possible to approximate surfaces like helicoids (Fig. 5.13) or conoids (Fig. 5.14) from elastic materials cut out and folded according to a pattern.

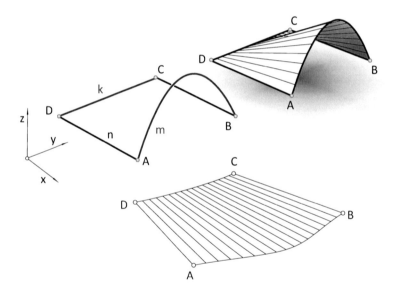

As previously said, making patterns for producing and cutting double curved surfaces may be reduced to the problem of approximating such surfaces by polyhedral ones which may be developed into a plane. A particularly interesting use of developable surfaces concerns the way in which they are employed to study procedures for generating complex shapes which are easy to realise or build. Very interesting compositions are made by perforating paper or veneer along curved lines and bending or folding the material along the perforation (Fig. 5.15).

Fig. 5.14 *Conoid*

Fig. 5.15 Paper sculptures, arch. Zaha Hadid, 13th International Architecture Exhibition – Common Graund, Venice, 2012

Minimal and free–form surfaces are two examples of other important curved surface types in architectural scale modelling. The most important characteristic of minimal surfaces is that they minimise the total surface area subject to a constraint.

This property made them highly popular in the second half of the 20th century. The weight and quantity of the material used when building such structures is reduced to a minimum. In terms of the geometric structure, different types of tensile structures are minimal surfaces (Fig. 5.16). It is easiest to scale model a minimal surface by "stretching" a highly elastic natural or synthetic material between supports. A minimal surface subject to a given constraint is obtained in this way.

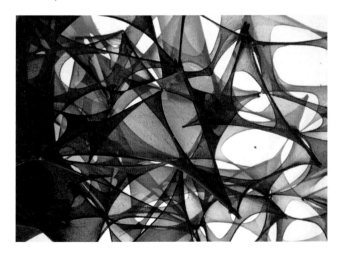

Fig. 5.16 Scale model of a tensile structure, 13th International Architecture Exhibition – Common Graund, Venice, 2012

The term free–form surfaces refers to complex geometric surfaces generated with sophisticated 3D geometric modelling tools operating with parametric curves known as spline curves. Spline modelling was first used in the aircraft and automotive industry, and it was only at the end of the 20th century that architects began to deploy it to create avant-garde architectural designs. Designs such as those made by Frank Gehry, Zaha Hadid, Bernhard Franken and other contemporary architects can only be generated with the use of the computer. Making a scale model or constructing an object which is, in geometry terms, a free–form surface is impossible using traditional construction methods; CAD/CAM technologies have to be used instead. The next chapter goes into more detail on ways to generate such shapes and make scale models based on information provided by digital models.

5.2   Preparation of the Components for Fabrication

After studying the design and selecting the size ratio, we may begin preparing the elements needed to fabricate the scale model. Today, a range of CAD software is used for this purpose, and it is recommended to draw, i.e. model the object to actual size and then readjust the scale during its fabrication. The amount of detail to be shown on the model will also depend on the selected size ratio.

The preparation of the components depends on the selected realisation technique. Basically, the model components may be prepared either for 3D printing or for cutting (laser, CNC machine or manual cutting).

3D printers are generally used to print designs of very complex shapes; basically, 3D printing is the only method which allows the transfer of complex geometry from the virtual to the physical world. The preparation of the components for 3D printing depends on the size of the printer used. An object whose size is no larger than 30x30x30cm may be printed as a single volume, whereas large objects must be split into parts which are joined together after the printing. No matter which CAD software is used to prepare the 3D model for printing, this should be done in a way to avoid having any self–intersecting surfaces. Also, all the edges of the 3D model must be closed (Fig. 5.17).

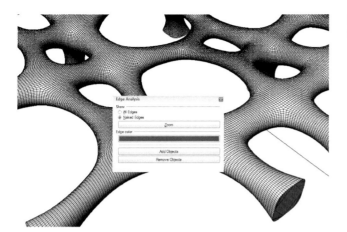

Fig. 5.17 3D model with closed edges

Achieving this, together with all the subsequent editing of the CAD model, may be quite tricky, and it usually takes a lot of patience to get the shapes right.

This software, which will vary according to the type of the 3D printer, is used to generate horizontal cross–sections. These sections are the path along which the head of the 3D printer moves (Fig. 5.18), setting down layers of the printing material to the required depths.

Preparing the components for cutting with a laser or CNC machine is far more demanding compared with the proce-dure explained above, as it requires dealing with a number of the scale model components simultaneously. With this type of preparation, several aspects must be taken into account concurrently: dividing the components into parts which can be joined together afterwards following a specific order, the thickness of the material, marking the compo-nents, the assembly, and identifying the accessory compo-nents which will help to put the scale model together.

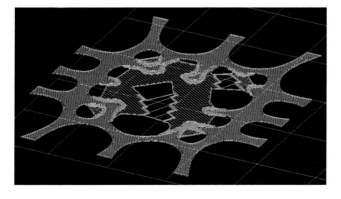

Fig. 5.18 Horizontal cross–section of the model

When employing this method, all meshes of the scale model must be developed on paper. When drawing the meshes, it is necessary to factor in the thickness of the material and the cutting width. To make the drawings the right size and shape, it is advisable to trial cut the material when beginning the preparation and then amend the drawings based on the obtained measurements. This type of fabrication requires the preparation of two–dimensional drawings, with different colours used to differentiate between different ways of processing the material (cutting, various engraving depths). It is recommended to use the layer structure, which helps deal with different types of components more easily. As a rule, non–standard objects will have a great number of similar components; it is thus very important to properly mark the connecting ones. In order to minimise the number of components that will be glued together, it is possible to engrave the material at places where such components adjoin and bend, or fold it after cutting (Fig. 5.19). It must be reiterated that this procedure will vary depending on the object being modelled. A corner of each component should be marked appropriately, preferably one that will remain hidden after the scale model has been joined together. When marking the components, it is recommended to use a multiple marking system, one which will specify the exact position of each component in three–dimensional space and in relation to the adjoining components. Sometimes, these marks are intentionally made in places where they will be visible after the assembly, becoming a part of the design and indicating the complexity of the scale model.

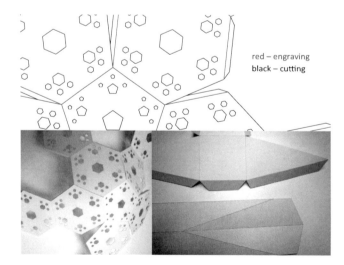

red – engraving
black – cutting

Fig. 5.19 *Line colour coding and engraving the material to allow folding*

After the components have been drawn, they are placed on the sheet to be cut (Fig. 5.20). It is recommended to connect the lines of the same kind (cutting lines, perforations, etc.) into a single object by making so–called polylines, which will allow uninterrupted laser movement and optimise the cutting process.

Since the components will often consist of several parts to be cut, engraved and/or designated, it is also recommended to group them together in order to not lose data while moving around the work space. When the elements have been grouped in this way, they are rearranged or rotated on the sheet of the material to be cut in order to come up with an arrangement that will result in minimum material waste.

If the chosen material cannot be cut with a laser cutter, it is prepared to be cut by hand. To mark the component contours, the previously made patterns are fixed on the material and control dots or the end points of the contour lines are marked by pressing the spike of a pair of compasses or a pin gently into the material along the pattern edges. Naturally, whether or not this technique may be used and how precise it is, will depend on the properties of the selected material (advisable to use with paperboard and wood, but not with plastics or sheet metal, which are prone to creasing and fracture). After marking the selected points on the material, these points or perforations are connected into lines with a ruler or curved ruler and a thin–lead pencil.

Fig. 5.20 *Two different kind of components laid out on a sheet of paper*

5.3   Cutting and Finishing

The materials used in scale modelling these days are mostly cut with laser cutters. Despite the common use of laser cutters, one must be familiar with manual cutting, which is a skill frequently needed in practice.

5.3.1   Manufacturing planar components

Sheets/boards/tables may be cut with a laser cutter or by hand. Depending on the type and power of the laser cutter, it may be used to cut materials as thick as 1.5 cm.

Before cutting the selected material, the power, speed and frequency of the laser beam must be adjusted accordingly. For this purpose, sample material should be cut first (see Chapter 4.2.1 for an in–depth explanation of how the laser works). All laser cutters operate within a range of values and must be set depending on the type and thickness of the material used. However, the materials used in scale modelling are most often produced locally and their physical properties may diverge significantly from the values specified by the laser manufacturer (in terms of density, moisture, etc.), necessitating additional adjustments. All cutting operations should thus be conducted on sample material before proceeding with the cutting of the actual components.

When setting the laser values, one must bear in mind what both faces of the material will look like after the cutting, or the depth to which the material will be engraved. When working with paperboard, one should make sure to adjust the laser beam so as to avoid leaving traces of cutting on either face, which may burn the edges. For instance, when it comes to engraving lines on paperboard, the penetration depth will depend on how visible we want the engraved line to be (Fig. 5.21).

When cutting plywood with a laser cutter, the cross–section along the cut is always darker than the faces of the material. This happens because maximum output power must be used to cut hard materials with a laser cutter, which tends to leave burn marks (Fig. 5.22).

Fig. 5.21 Cardboard engraving and various penetration depths

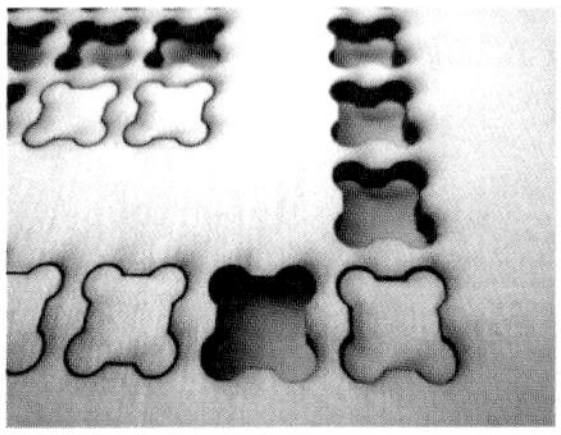

The latest types of lasers may be used for 3D cutting. 3D cutting makes it possible to cut sheet materials at arbitrary angles (Fig. 5.23). This is particularly helpful when it comes to joining together components with sheet materials of various thicknesses.

The width of the cut made with a laser cutter will depend on the type and thickness of the material used. Plastic materials melt fast under the laser beam, resulting in wider cut widths which may measure between 0.5 and 1.5 mm. When preparing the components for cutting, the cut width must be taken into account to ensure they are cut to the specified dimensions.

When thick plexiglass is cut with a laser cutter, the face of the cut is conical in shape because it is impossible to focus the laser beam. The laser cutter is usually adjusted with the upper face of the material in mind, which basically makes it impossible to have the same focus on both sides. On the other hand, this property may be advantageous when engraving the material. If the laser beam is focused above the surface of the material, it will make a broad cut (Fig. 5.24).

Fig. 5.22 Cutting marks on plywood

Fig. 5.23 Laser cutting at arbitrary angles and its application in scale modelling

Since laser cutting tends to leave marks on the material, components are often cut manually instead. In such cases, material remnants are used to laser cut patterns which are then used to cut the material by hand. To cut paper, cardboard, veneer or balsa manually, a pattern ruler is placed along the cutting line on the side of the material which will be visible after the assembly. This is done as a precaution and for safety reasons, in order to prevent the scalpel knife from straying accidentally and cuting into the edge of the material. The scalpel blade should be sharp at all times, because a blunt blade may easily scratch or jag the material. The scalpel blade should be positioned at an angle no greater than 45 degrees to the cutting surface; the scalpel should first be pulled gently, without pressing hard, to make a shallow cut in the material.

Fig. 5.24 *Different cuts; a conical cross–section; engraving*

The cut should extend somewhat beyond the end points of the cutting line. If the material is thick or hard, the scalpel should be pulled gently along the cutting line several times, until it has cut through the material. For the perpendicular cutting of veneer or balsa to the annual rings, exceptionally sharp scalpel blades are used. The scalpel is positioned at a sharp angle to the surface of the material (approx. 30°), pressed gently against the material and pulled repeatedly until it has cut through it. When cutting out openings, the material is first pierced along the opening perimeter and a cut is made from one point to the next. By doing so, one will avoid running the scalpel blade beyond the opening perimeter.

A special type of plastic cutting tool called the scriber is used to cut plastic foil or solid plastic boards. Different scribers are used for different types of plastic, as specified by the scriber manufacturer (Fig. 5.25).

Cutting paper, foil and veneer along curved lines is usually done with scissors. Roll scalpels, or scalpels with thin, sharp blades are needed when working with thin cardboard or balsa. Roll scalpels may be used in combination with curved rulers, which are placed on the material along the line of the curve.

Fig. 5.25 *Scriber cutting*

A scalpel with a blade angle of 45 degrees should be used to cut a thick material at a 45–degree angle (Fig. 5.26). This type of scalpel is used in a way similar to how common

scalpels are used: it is placed against the edge of the ruler and parallel to the cutting line, with its tip touching the end point of the line. The blade is then pressed slightly into the material and the scalpel pulled gently to the end of the cutting line. The cutting movement is repeated several times, with the blade pressing deeper into the material each time until it has cut through it.

Fig. 5.26 *Cutting with a 45–degree blade angle scalpel*

After the components have been cut out, they are filed or sanded with sandpaper of the right grit to remedy any defects caused during the cutting (e.g., a jagged, zigzagging line, from using a blunt blade, or from cutting the material with an unsteady hand at an angle deviating from 90 degrees). To correct the defects, the components are carefully sanded to avoid removing too much material, as this might spoil joining the scale model together. Files are usually used to smoothen openings, both circular and rectangular (Fig. 5.27).

Fig. 5.27 *Filing and sanding cutouts*

Jig saws and hand saws are used to cut plywood along curved lines. When cutting thick wooden boards along curved lines (e.g., MDF), narrow, spaced–out holes are first bored along the cutting line with an electric drill using a wood bit. A jig saw is then used to cut between the holes. Hardboard may also be cut immediately with a jig saw, but operating it with precision and accuracy requires some experience. The cut components are then finished with a file or sandpaper. Special tools are used for cutting materials such as plexiglass, glass, etc. along curved lines (e.g., electric hand saws with plexiglass blades, diamond knives for cutting glass, etc.).

Cutting rods and wire depends on the type of the material they are made of, their shape and size. Rods with a circular or a rectangular cross–section are most often cut at an angle with a mitre saw. The mitre box is fastened to the work surface with a pair of clamps, with enough space left to place the material and manipulate it during the cutting. Next, the material is placed in the mitre box and cut with a hand saw (different hand saws are used with different materials) (Fig. 5.28). The mitre box has notches on both sides to insert saw blades at 90– and 45–degree angles. Small mitre boxes often come equipped with a saw with a fixed wood cutting blade. Wire is cut with different kinds of pincers and pliers. After cutting a rod, its ends should also be filed or sanded.

Fig. 5.28 *Cutting a rod with a hand saw in a mitre box*

5.4   Gluing the Components

After the components have been cut out and sanded, they are glued together. Since scale model components are commonly made of different materials, they should be glued with a universal adhesive. Universal adhesives glue different materials without causing chemical damage or changing their colour, stability, and other basic characteristics.

Regardless of what is being glued, one should make sure no traces of the adhesive are left on surfaces that will be visible on the completed scale model. This is achieved by applying a thin layer of glue in a controlled manner. The adhesive should be squeezed carefully from the tube, which is first moved slightly away from the edge being glued, and then applied in a thin layer. This makes it possible to ensure the layer is not thicker than it should be and does not smear. The extra glue should be carefully removed. Still, if it leaks or smears, it should be scraped when dry and the joined components sanded to a fine finish.

When gluing paper, cardboard or plastic foil, if the adhesive leaks or smears and cannot be removed by sanding the components, they should be cut and glued again. Canister spray adhesives allow even application and should thus be used when gluing large surfaces. For large surfaces to be glued properly, they must be clamped or pressed under something heavy until the adhesive has dried out. This is done so the cardboard does not crease and stays firm and even.

Gluing plexiglass/acrylic sheets: adhesives which do not leave traces are used most frequently. The protective foil is peeled off the material just before applying the adhesive to keep the surface of the acrylic board clean. In case there are traces of dirt on it, it should be cleaned with a damp and soft cloth before applying the glue. While sticking the components, tweezers are used or gloves worn in order to not leave fingerprints on the material.

Gluing wood: special wood adhesives are used. First, the edges of the material to be glued should be cleaned. After the adhesive has been applied and the components stuck, they must be clamped to stick firmly. After pressing the components together, some glue is likely to come out, which should be carefully removed before it dries.

In scale modelling, window and door openings are most often covered with transparent plastic foil (coloured or colourless) to represent glass. The foil cutouts should be larger in size than the actual openings. The adhesive is applied from a slight distance along the edge of the wall of the opening, not on the foil, and then spread in a thin layer. Next, the foil cutout is carefully attached, without too much movement, to avoid adhesive smearing. In case this happens, the adhesive should be carefully removed with a sharp scalpel knife to avoid damaging the foil. If there are bars/mullions in the openings (windows usually have them), they are added only after the foil has stuck firmly to the support. The adhesive is applied in small blobs on the bar/mullion, spread with a finger and carefully placed in the required/designated position with a pair of tweezers.

Fig. 5.29 *Different ways of gluing walls joining at right angles*

When gluing the components of a staircase together, the step treads are stuck to the previously cut stair stringers one by one. This is done with a pair of tweezers, which is used to hold each tread while applying a thin layer of the adhesive along its edge through the tube opening. The treads are stuck to the stringers at their designated places. Each tread should be held with the tweezers until the glue has dried.

Before gluing the external walls of rectangular buildings together, the wall edges are cut at a 45–degree angle (Fig. 5.29), and those of polygonal buildings are cut along the centrelines of the angles between the walls. To help glue the walls, a pattern or bracket may be made from a thick material, which is used to brace or strengthen the wall connection. Similar angular supports may be made and placed on the inside of the walls to reinforce the structure.

5.5   Assembly and Final Processing

Assembly is the final stage of the scale model realisation. During this stage, all the previously manufactured components of the scale model are joined together, coordinated and fixed. This stage also involves the final processing of the model. When putting the components together, attention must be paid to every single detail or piece, its position in terms of function, spatial arrangement and connection with the other components, while maintaining precision and orderliness and bearing the effects the model is intended to produce in mind. Like everything else in scale modelling, the assembly should be done according to a procedure. Thus, the main object of the scale model and its parts or ancillary items are placed first, i. e. fixed or glued to the base. Then all the other objects are added (accessory buildings/objects), followed by the embellishing details which are placed last (vegetation, street furniture, infrastructure, etc.).

Painting is part of the final processing of the scale model. It may be very complicated to paint the completed scale model, and quite often it is better not to paint it at all and keep the original colour of the material used. The entire model or only some parts of it may be painted. Before painting the scale model, it should be prepared relative to the material it is made from and the paint to be used. The preparation for painting has several stages: the scale model is first sanded; next, putty is applied where necessary, after which it is sanded again; finally, an undercoating is applied (primer), followed by a layer of the finish paint. Paint is applied with brushes, rollers, spray canisters and pressure pots. Before using paint, it is advisable to test the scale model and see how it reacts, to make sure the material does not corrode after exposure to it and the colour does not change after drying.

City models and landscape models often contain bodies of water such as lakes, streams, rivers, sea shores, or simply outdoor pools. The most commonly used technique to represent such elements which is also the easiest, is using a sheet material whose texture, colour and reflection properties will distinguish it from the rest of the surfaces depicted on the terrain on the scale model. Reflective materials or transparent foil (shiny transparent plastic foil, aluminium foil, ribbed fabric, etc.) are the most frequently used materials.

Bodies of water may be modelled with epoxy resin. The bed of the river, lake, pool, etc. is made first when preparing the scale model for the application of epoxy resin. Other objects are put along/in the bed, such as sand, moss, pebbles, reed, etc. The bed may also be painted, following the principle that the greater the depth of the water, the less visible the bed, which means darker shades should be used for greater depths. It is easiest to apply combinations of navy blue, brown or grey tempera, using lighter shades as one approaches the bank or shore.

Once the bed has been prepared (including the gluing of extra objects) and is dry, it is covered with epoxy resin. Epoxy resin is sold colourless or in different colours, in form of granules or as two–component putty. Granular epoxy resin is heated to temperatures between 150–200°C to make sure the mass is uniform. It takes 4–5 minutes to dry, but this short drying time nonetheless allows the material to be shaped to create different effects (rough water, ripples, etc.). Two–component epoxy resin putty is also homogenised first, poured and left to dry. Its drying time is longer, allowing more time to finish the surface, which makes it suitable for large surfaces.

When assembling city models or site models, it is common to fix all the objects comprising the particular urban complex or site to on the base first. As needed, those objects are painted the same colour, e.g. white, using a pressure pot, after which the infrastructure, vegetation and other details are coloured; lastly, the scale model of the main or the building to be constructed is put in its position. This manner of presentation helps to highlight the building, and thanks to its materials and colouring, it will stand out amongst the other elements of the model.

Quite often, final work also involves installing various man–made environment objects to show the scale of the building. Bas–relief paper, coloured paper or fabric covered with artificial grass may be used to imitate grass. Also, grass may be replaced with ready–made modelling materials of grass–like structure, which may be coloured green or a light, neutral colour to match the palette of the scale model. Any other material at hand, such as little rocks or sand, may also be used when making a scale model, along with the ready–made items sold in model kit shops, such as human figures, different kinds of low and tall vegetation, street furniture (benches, cars), etc.

When making site models for design competitions, space is left on the model in which the scale models of the proposed designs can be inserted later. The models accompanying competition entries are then temporarily inserted in the site model to allow the jury to see the designs on the same terms, in the context of the surroundings or broader urban setting. This helps the jury select the best design based on the physical models of the designs and not their virtual representations, which may be misleading in many respects.

Lighting the scale model (Fig. 5.30) is also done as part of the final processing. Interior or exterior lighting may be installed to light a model.

Fig. 5.30 *Scale model lighting: Fiat Car factory Kragujevac, modelArt studio*

Lighting is used to create special effects and highlight parts of the scale model. Interior lighting and its necessary components (batteries, light–emitting diodes/LEDs, switches and wiring) are installed so as to be hidden, easily replaceable, and contribute maximally to the visual appeal of the scale model. The on/off switch should be installed at the side of the model so it is both hard to notice and easy to reach.

The LEDs inside the object should be arranged in a way that makes the lighting as effective as possible, as well as to maximise the overall similarity of the model to the actual building. Likewise, the exterior of the model may be lit using various kinds of lamp posts or floodlights arranged and directed to discreetly light the front/facades of the main object or building.

The lighting of the model and the related technical details should be planned in the early stages of the modelling process. As a result, it may be necessary to choose or adapt the components of the model to suit the lighting purposes (e.g., by using matte foil insted of a transparent material to represent glass, or a reflective material instead of matte foil, etc.). In any case, lighting a model effectively requires careful planning and even more careful realisation, given how much it may contribute to the overall effect of the completed scale model and the impression it makes.

5.6   Presentation of Scale Models

The purpose and relevance of a scale model is only seen after it has been put on display. Important buildings usually have their scale models displayed in their halls, and their purpose is to show the visitors the shape/design and use of the building. In such cases, the way in which the scale model is displayed has been planned carefully beforehand, and it is usually part of a large–scale presentation consisting of printed materials, posters, screenings, verbal presentations, etc. The model is put in a glass or plexiglass showcase to protect it from outside impact and damage. Sometimes, scale models are made for educational purposes and are not put in showcases so the visitors may touch them. In such cases, the lifespan of the scale model is much shorter and it must be replaced after some time.

5.6.1   Transport

The place where the scale model is to be displayed is often not the same as that where it was created, which means it might need transporting to the designated location. In order not to damage the scale model during transport, special protective packaging must be used. The type of packaging will depend on the type of transport.

Before dispatching the scale model over a relatively long distance by public transport, heavy duty packaging is chosen and produced in which the model is fixed and protected against potential impact, shock or tumbles. Depending on the characteristics of the scale model, it may be necessary to produce a special frame in which the model is firmly secured before transport, as is the case with tall objects. This is absolutely necessary as there is danger of the scale model suffering damage due to movement during transport, which may affect its overall integrity. This support frame should be designed and constructed along with the fabrication of the scale model so it can be used more than just once (this concerns scale models that will be displayed in touring exhibitions).

Once the scale model has been placed and secured in a specially made wooden box and protected additionally with expanded polystyrene beads or air–filled cushions, it is necessary to specify on the outside of the box that its contents are fragile and breakable to prevent the scale model being damaged due to rocking or tumbling during transport.

A more expensive transport option would be hiring a firm specialising in fine art shipping. In that case, the firm collects the scale model and is in charge of its packing, shipment and delivery. As a rule, these firms insure the items to be transported and obtain all the required shipment, customs and other paperwork. With this option, the risk of the scale model being damaged during transport is reduced to a minimum.

If possible, it is advisable to inspect the integrity of the scale model upon its arrival and reinforce it or repair any potential defects.

5.6.2   Lighting and other presentation media

After the scale model has been conveyed to the venue where it will be permanently displayed, it must be properly prepared for presentation.

When a scale model is put on display in the building it represents, it is usually placed in its hall, with plenty of daylight or additional lighting, and in an easily accessible place, where visitors can see it from all sides. From time to time, it is necessary to "freshen it up" or replace some of its components. Most often, it is the protective plexiglass showcase that needs replacing, along with the interior lighting of the model, where it exists. Quite commonly, the items and objects surrounding the scale model are changed in accordance with the changes to the actual site or grounds (if new buildings and transportation facilities have been built in the meantime), necessitating extensive works to upgrade the site model.

Lighting the scale model effectively is part of the overall presentation strategy. Exhibiting a bright–coloured model furnished with exterior or interior lighting in a room full of light, and displaying a dark–coloured model in a dark room will definitely create different effects. Therefore, the scale model builder should be familiar with the conditions in the room where the model will be shown and make sure, where possible, the display conditions are adjusted to suit the model and are as close to ideal as possible. This aspect is hard to predict; therefore, it is best to act according to the circumstances while preparing the scale model for presentation and to try and readjust the setting to make it as effective as possible. Quite often, it is necessary to install extra lighting; in such situations, it is best to have ceiling lighting, as it does not cast large, unnatural shadows on the model and minimises the shadows made by the visitors.

Finally, as previously suggested, each scale model must have an information plate on it with the basic data about the building, investor, architect/designer, scale, year of production and the name of the modelling studio or builder(s) of the model. This information plate should be put in a discreet and yet visible place, on the front or the side of the scale model, where it is easy to see and read. Once the information plate has been installed and the model put on display, it begins to live its second, public life, and to develop a personal identity.

Scale models of broader central city zones are often placed in the pedestrian precincts of city cores, historical and otherwise. These models are typically cast in bronze and fixed on permanent pediments at eye level. There is usually an indication of the exact position of the scale model in the city core for the visitors to be able to position themselves in relation to various landmarks by observing the model and its immediate surroundings. Such scale models are often part of a city's tourist inventory and are of interest to first–time visitors. They are also a great help when finding one's way around. Because of the properties of the materials they are made of, these scale models are not damaged by outdoor weather. They are additionally lit at night, making attractive gathering points for the city's inhabitants and visitors alike.

5.6.3   Photographing scale models

Completed scale models are photographed for two common reasons. The first is to build up an archive, as nowadays scale model builders and modelling studios generally have digital catalogues of their models, often web–based, which bring them new commissions. The second has to do with the preparation of photographic material for printing and publication, which is then used to present or promote the scale model and the building or structure it represents for various purposes (promotion of the building, market sales, tourist offer, technology presentation, etc.) and to different audiences or consumers.

The photographs should be of the highest possible quality. They should be taken in a professional manner, for which every modelling studio should be adequately equipped. Basic photographic equipment comprises a high–resolution/high–pixel camera, a set of interchangeable lenses, additional lighting (floodlights with stands, coloured filters and a power generator), and a neutral backdrop (black, gray or white). It is vital to plan photographing the scale model beforehand, as the process will vary depending on the type of the model. Town scale models are photographed in conditions different from those needed to show a technological process. Thus, before taking photos of the scale model, it is necessary to decide on the desired outcomes and choose the lighting and lenses accordingly. How the scale model is captured on film also depends on its exterior/interior lighting, the size of its surfaces, height, brightness, whether it is made of glass or wood, which all plays a part in deciding on the best way to make pictures of it.

Scale models are photographed in two stages. In the first stage, the model is prepared for photographing, together with the backdrop and lighting. It is placed on the selected base or against the selected backdrop and lit with floodlights to control the shadows cast by the objects or items on the model and on the base or backdrop. To do this, the floodlights are moved and readjusted, in order to make the shadows discreet and not too strong. To get the best results, the lighting should resemble natural daylight as much as possible. The model is photographed in the second stage. This can be done with a hand–held camera, at high speeds for optimum sharpness, or from a stand. Photographing the model with a hand–held camera allows variations and may result in unexpectedly good shots, but also in blurred ones. On the other hand, using a camera on a tripod requires choosing an angle from which the highest–quality pictures will be obtained in advance. Naturally, it is possible to vary the shooting angle, as well as to reposition the scale model against the lighting to take new pictures. As a rule, the entire model is photographed first, showing all of its components together. For this purpose, standard camera lenses are used (e.g., 55 mm). To photograph details of the facade or the interior, special lenses are used, such as wide–angle lenses (e.g., 20 mm) and tele–lenses (e.g., 150 mm). The lenses are selected depending on the desired effects. Human figures that are generally not part of the finished models are inserted to show the relative size of the scale model in the photographs. They are placed in such positions as to resemble the actual conditions of the site or building and are used merely as temporary decoration. It may take a long time to take pictures of a scale model, but the process can be quite engrossing and lead to unexpectedly good photos, if carefully planned. To take good photographs, one needs experience in both setting the scene and operating the equipment.

The photographs taken may be edited later using photo editing software. The best photographs of the scale model are selected and specially prepared depending on how they will be used. They are often made ready for catalogues, promotional material or posters/billboards, which involves their preparation for publishing, printing or plotting. Sometimes, photographs are used to show the model online, for which special preparation is needed. A similar treatment is required when using the photographs of a model to illustrate a verbal presentation, which are then shown with a video projector or beam. As digital image editing is not the subject of this book, it will not be discussed here in detail.

In the next chapter, we deal with using digital technologies to generate computer models, as well as with various contemporary production methods.

References:

[1] Pottmann, H., Asperl, A., Hofer, M., Kilian, A.: Architectural Geometry. Bentley Institute Press (2007)

[2] Troche, C.: Planar hexagonalmeshes by tangent plane Intersection. In: Advances in Architectural Geometry, Vienna, 13–16 September 2008

[3] Wang, W., Liu, Y.: A note on planar hexagonal meshes. In: Emirisl. Z, Sottile F. , Theobald,T. (eds.) Nonlinear computational Geometry, vol.151, pp. 221–233. Springer, New York (2010)

[4] Wang, W., Liu, Y., Yan, D., Chan, B., Ling, R., Sun, F.: Hexagonal meshes with planarfaces. In: Technical Report, TR–2008–13, University of Hong Kong (2008)

[5] Zadravec, M., Schiftner, A., Wallner, J.: Designing quad–dominant meshes with planar faces. In: Sorkine O., Levy B.(eds.)Eurographics Symposium on Geometry Processing, Lyon (2010)

6 DIGITAL TECHNOLOGY SOFTWARE USED FOR ARCHITECTURAL MODELLING

6 DIGITAL TECHNOLOGY SOFTWARE USED FOR ARCHITECTURAL MODELLING

Practically all stages of architectural design and construction have been revolutionised by digital technology, including scale modelling. One aspect which is particularly relevant for model building is the possibility of manufacturing entire models or parts of models using information generated from digital 3D models. Digital fabrication allows the building of geometrically complex objects which are impossible or very difficult to realise using traditional model building techniques. At the same time, it has opened up possibilities for exploring new geometric shapes whose aesthetic quality and functional properties may be inspected and verified not only with computer–generated 3D models, but also with digitally fabricated physical models. The size and geometric properties of a model and the material used for its fabrication are the key factors to be considered when opting for a software application and a digital fabrication method. This chapter offers more detailed instructions on how to use model–generating software and digital fabrication techniques.

Digital fabrication refers to the methods used to manufacture models, replicas and prototypes of buildings or objects based on digitally generated information. Digital fabrication is closely related to CAD/CAM technologies. The acronyms CAD/CAM (computer–aided design/computer–aided manufacturing) refer to the computer systems technology used for digital design and fabrication. Digital fabrication technologies were originally developed for the needs of industrial design and mechanical engineering, shipbuilding and marine engineering, as well as automotive and aviation industries, but they are also increasingly used in architecture. A growing number of architects employ digital fabrication techniques during the investigating stage of their projects to realise geometrically complex models, and also to fabricate parts of buildings or structures. The material, size and geometric properties of the building or object that needs to be fabricated influence the choice of the technology and process of fabrication.

CAD/CAM technologies were first utilised in the mid–20th century, with the advent of CNC (computer numerical control) machines. The first CNC machines were designed for the needs of the U.S. military industry, but they found application in industrial design as early as the 1960s. CAD/CAM technologies were first employed in the automotive and aviation industries. In the early 1990s, the first architectural designs benefited from both these technologies and digital fabrication. One of the earliest fully digitally generated and fabricated design– was the fish sculpture by architect Frank Gehry (Barcelona, 1992). By the end of the 1990s, more buildings were constructed using CAD/CAM and CNC fabrication, of which The Guggenheim Museum Bilbao is probably the best known. Rapid prototyping (RP) machines used for digital fabrication are a more recent innovation, developed in the late 1980s and in the 1990s; they are used more exclusively for the fabrication of prototypes and models [4]. These various digital fabrication technologies are fundamentally different from one another and require varying approaches to model generation and fabrication as well as material processing/preparation, which is why they are discussed in greater detail below. As this book focuses specifically on the 3D modelling and digital fabrication of architectural scale models, this discussion is limited only to those methods and software used for manufacturing scale models.

Before a more detailed explanation of digital fabrication follows, here is an overview of the variety of software used to generate architectural scale models.

6.1   Computer Modelling Software – An Overview

Digital modelling software has by now been introduced and fully embraced by architects – one–person studios as well as those employing teams of architects – and is used for the design of small and large projects alike. The reason for this general acceptance of the software resulting from the mergence of CAD/CAM technologies and computer graphics is the wide array of modelling, rendering and animation functions it commonly offers. Another advantage is that it allows direct transfer of information to CNC or RP machines for model fabrication.

A variety of architectural design software is utilised for design development. Preliminary designs typically differ significantly from concepts, a fact which bears direct relevance to what an architect might need; accordingly, different applications are used in the different stages of design development. Practically, there is no single application that supports all the discrete stages of the process, forcing architects to use a range of software when working on a design.

6.1.1　Conceptual Modelling Software

In the first stage of design (conceptual design) architects make sketches, which they use to transfer their concepts into a virtual CAD environment. No precise mathematical modelling is done at this stage; rather, it concerns visualising the concept of the object and studying spatial relations. During this stage it is very important to examine the physical properties of the material that will be used, which can only be done by building a scale model. This is why it is essential to use software with simple functions which allows intuitive modelling. Listed below are some architectural design programs suitable for 3D modelling, which are also used to export information for digital fabrication.

SketchUp is a polygonal modelling software application, which is convenient because it allows fast intuitive 3D modelling, quite similar to working with pen and paper [6]. Principally, the program uses geometric shapes for building spatial elements. For example, a straight line is generated by connecting two points, a plane by connecting three points, and two–dimensional shapes are extruded to become three–dimensional. As the cursor moves across the user interface screen, it recognises the planes that define shapes or objects and allows the insertion of more 2D or 3D shapes in those planes. Spatial transformations like translation, rotation and mirroring are linked to the copy, array and scale functions to facilitate modelling. All elements in the SketchUp environment are represented as a series of rectilinear elements, i.e., corresponding polygons, a limiting factor when it comes to generating flat surfaces, which gives competitive advantage to other environments which use mathematical algorithms. While the program is highly intuitive to use, all its functions may also be numerically controlled. It has a repository of models/model assemblies and plug–ins that are downloadable from the Internet. Also, its models may directly be loaded in Google Earth. The software was designed and marketed by @Last Software, Inc, Colorado, U.S. in 1999, acquired by Google in 2007 and has been part of Trimble since 2012. It has been available in two versions since then: as a free product and as payware (SkechUp Pro). The main difference between the two is the possibility of importing models from and exporting them to various fabrication formats offered in SkechUp Pro.

AutoCAD is a 2D drawing and 3D modelling software application most commonly used in architecture. It is based on polygonal modelling, but the latest versions also allow NURBS modelling as part of the 3D modelling suite (although limited). AutoCAD Architecture offers many functions specially suited to architectural work, such as the automatic generation of two–dimensional drawings of arbitrarily selected cross–sections and elevations of an object, or building, based on a 3D model [1]. It is used for conceptual modelling, and modellers mostly use it to generate 2D drawings for laser cutting.

Rhinoceros or Rhino is a commercial 3D modelling software package. It is NURBS–based, with shapes or elements defined exclusively as mathematical representations. The advantage of NURBS–oriented software is that considerably less information is needed to generate a shape, in comparison with that based on polygonal modelling. Recently, Rhinoceros has been the prime choice of architects for designing non–standard objects. This software may be used for all stages of design, from concept modelling to generating working designs ready for fabrication. Its comparative popularity stems from its diversity, as it may be used to generate a complete range of shapes, to edit and analyse NURBS elements, and it also has the capability to accurately transfer 3D geometry between applications for fabrication and other purposes. Rhinoceros was developed and marketed by the Seattle–based U.S. company Robert McNeel & Associates [3].

Except for the applications discussed above, computer–generated imagery software (CGI) such as 3ds Max, Maya and Cinema 4D is often used for design development. The listed applications were developed for the needs of the film and video game industries, so understandably they do not offer functions needed specifically by architects/engineers. Nonetheless, they do meet their needs when investigating and manipulating shapes in the stage of conceptual modelling (mainly those with curved surfaces). CGI software may be used to simulate the behaviour of a building or object in real 3D space, such as under the influence of gravity, wind impact, fluid dynamics, movement of particles, etc. CGI software applications differ in terms of the specialised tools they offer; for instance, 3ds Max has better mesh modelling functions, whereas Maya offers a wider array of NURBS tools. A variety of plug–ins are also used to extend the basic suites of these software applications. As well as that, special software has been developed to meet special needs, some of which may find application in architecture. For example, ZBrush is primarily used for digital sculpting, but it may also be used in architectural design and scale modelling to add organic details to the basic model to make its appearance bio–morphological.

6.1.2   Parametric Modelling Software

Parametric modelling refers to generating entities using parameters. The majority of software applications used for architectural modelling today have some parametric modelling functions and tools (macros, script, plug–ins, etc.). Parametric modelling in the age of non–standard architecture is gaining popularity among architectural professionals due to its unlimited possibilities when generating and analysing shapes and models. This kind of design is generally used in the stage of conceptual form analysis. Parametric definitions may be used to connect design development to fabrication, thus optimising the overall process of architectural scale modelling.

Most 3D software applications offer additional modelling possibilities through the use of scripts. Rhinoceros has two parametric modelling tools, RhinoScript and Grasshopper. RhinoScript is a scripting tool, which requires basic knowledge of programming, and solid operational knowledge of Rhinoceros for optimal application use. Grasshopper is a visual programing language plug–in with programming functions grouped into pre–programming modules called canvases. This allows the user with limited programming skills to learn the basics of parametric design. Along with canvases, the language allows the possibility of generating elements based on Rhinoceros modelling and offers mathematical functions that can be used to define new relations between objects. Modelling geometrically complex shapes requires solid operational knowledge of both geometry and programming (programming in C# and VB). The tight integration of Grasshopper with Rhino's modelling tools is the reason why it is more popular than RhinoScript, with a large user community contributing to its continuous upgrading.

Maya offers the possibility of parametric representation through the use of Maya Mel. Basic knowledge of programming is needed to use this scripting tool efficiently, and architects and designers typically use it in the stage of conceptual modelling to animate changes as they experiment with different shapes. Similarly, the capabilities of 3ds Max are augmented with Maxscript. Additionally, both applications offer modifiers, conventional tools that can also be used for parametric modelling.

The SketchUp suite contains the Ruby Console, which is an environment used for parametric representation. Cinema 4D also offers an additional tool called COFFEE used for parametric modelling. Nowadays, many architects use open–source programming languages and processing environments to generate 3D entities and their interactions. The great number of parametric modelling applications and tools available today indicate that they will continue to be upgraded and that many more are likely to be developed in the future.

6.2   CNC Digital Fabrication

CNC (Computer Numerical Control) is a method for the electronic setting and operation of machines. Computer operated machines are thus known as CNC machines. This method is used to convert 2D shapes and 3D models into a language understood by machines. Basically, CNC machines differ according to the machining method used, which is either subtractive or additive. Subtractive machining refers to machining an object out of a piece or block of a sheet or volumetric material, and is the digital fabrication method most frequently used in scale modelling. Additive machining refers to layering a material to produce a 3D model, and is also known as rapid prototyping.

The machines used for CNC fabrication may also be classified according to the number of degrees of freedom of movement. The number of degrees of freedom refers to the capability of a rigid body to move along and rotate about the x, y or z axes. Practically, the maximum number of degrees of freedom is six, with three components of translation and three components of rotation. Most machines used for digital fabrication have only two degrees of freedom, i.e., they can move in the x and y directions, and are used for cutting and processing sheet materials. Because these machines only cut in the xy plane, this method is also known as 2D CNC fabrication.

Cutting sheet materials is the simplest CNC machining operation. As previously said, sheet materials are materials whose thickness is relatively or negligibly small relative to their length and width. The thickness of sheet materials may range from one–tenth of a millimetre to several centimetres. They are cut with laser and plasma cutters, water–jet cutting machines and CNC machining centres. Which of these cutting techniques is selected and whether CNC machining is the method of choice principally depends on the thickness and hardness of the material and its melting point, i.e., its flammability.

Water jet cutting is used with materials whose physical and chemical properties do not change when they come into contact with water. Water jets are tools capable of cutting into a material using a concentrated, high–velocity jet of water, which is released through a high–pressure inlet. This technique is used to cut hard materials like steel, glass, concrete and granite (Fig. 6.1). The width or kerf of the cut made with a water jet depends on whether an abrasive (e.g., sand) is used in combination with water. Water alone is used to cut relatively soft materials, with cut kerfs as small as 0.07 mm, which is approximately the breadth of a human hair. With the addition of an abrasive element, the cut width increases to approximately 1 mm, allowing the cutting of very hard materials such as concrete and steel. One downside of this technology is the difficulty of precision cuts in thick materials.

Fig. 6.1 *Scale model fabricated using a water jet cutter. Project Marbel, A–cero Architects, 2006*

CNC routers are milling machines with two and a half degrees of freedom used to machine both sheet and volumetric materials. They come in different sizes, with process lengths and widths ranging from small (500 mm) to big (20,000 mm). They may be used for a variety of operations, such as 3D milling, 2D cutting, drilling, area clearing (similar to engraving), and text or pattern engraving. The possibility of machining very small elements with CNC routers depends on the smallest tool available to the modeller. The maximum tool length and the required degree of machining precision limit the maximum thickness of the material to be cut or processed. CNC routers are used to machine a variety of materials, such as metal, wood, acrylic glass, polystyrene foam, plastics and glass. This is a subtractive method and only one face of the material may be machined at a time. The material must be rotated 180° along a horizontal axis to process or cut it along both surfaces (Fig. 6.2).

Fig. 6.2 *Faces and a cross–section of a model CNC machined along the upper and bottom surfaces*

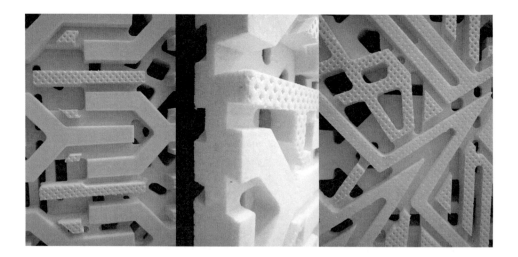

CNC milling machines are most frequently used by modellers to build terrain models. In principle, a model is machined out of a piece or block of material, which means extra material is removed by the router. Machining is consistent with the numerically controlled movement of the router tool. An example is given below in which the basic terms and principles of CNC machining are explained. They are essential to understand how to avoid damaging the machine and/or the material and to optimise fabrication.

Fig. 6.3 shows a digitally–generated relief model ready for fabrication. The size of the material block is selected based on the size of the terrain, and it should be 2 cm larger than the model to allow for edges. The material is fixed into a frame prior to fabrication to keep it from moving. This may be done in different ways as long as the block is stabilised on five sides (the lateral sides are fixed to a frame and the bottom is stuck to a base with double–sided adhesive tape). The edges are cut off at the end or after the fabrication, depending on whether the model will be transported immediately.

The tool should be selected relative to the material. The stepdown, which is how deep the tool goes, also depends on the type of the material as well as the size of the tool itself. When machining soft materials, the stepdown may equal the total flute length of the tool, but it should only be a fraction of it when working with hard materials, making it necessary to repeat the passes. When generating a tool path, it is necessary to specify the distance the tool will move horizontally when making the next pass. This distance, known as the stepover, may not exceed the total diameter of the tool.

Fig. 6.3 Terrain model showing the machining toolpaths

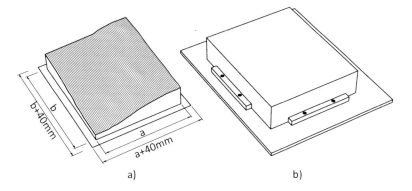

a)   b)

Fabrication is done in several stages. Fig. 6.4 shows a cross–section of a terrain and the individual stages of the machining operation. If the depth of the cut is greater than the stepdown, the upper layer of the material is machined first (Fig. 6.4a), followed by the second in the next stage (Fig. 6.4b). Depending on the precision and smoothness required for the completed model, the surface is finished with a fine tool to make it smoother (Fig. 6.4c). At the end of the process, the vertical edges of the model may be cut off manually. After the model has been machined out, it may be necessary to finish it by hand with sandpaper or a file.

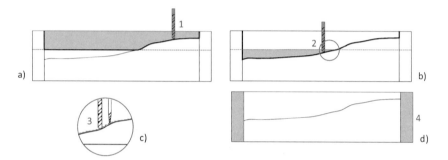

Fig. 6.5 shows a CNC milling machine in operation and a detail with a milling tool.

Fig. 6.4 Main machining steps

Fig. 6.6a shows a terrain model generated by roughing (prior to or with no finishing passes). Fig. 6.6b shows a model finished to a precise form, and Fig. 6.6c and Fig. 6.6d a model which was spray painted after machining, which also demonstrates the high level of precision achieved using this method.

Fig. 6.5 CNC milling machine (left); a detail showing a milling tool (right)

Machines with several degrees of freedom allow greater flexibility in model fabrication, but they are extremely expensive and are thus not commonly used for scale modelling. There are CNC milling machines with five or more degrees of freedom, as well as robot arms with more than six degrees of freedom (Fig. 6.7).

Fig. 6.6 *Various relief models generated by CNC milling*

Fig. 6.7 *Cutting a part out of an EPS block with hot wire controlled by a robot arm*

This technology has been used by some industries for more than 70 years, but it is still not very common in architecture. The robot arm may be employed for machining a block of material by removing layer after layer on any side and at any angle to realise the model (Fig. 6.8). When machines with several degrees of freedom are used, the end product is usually a finished model, a sculpture or a doubly curved prefabricated part or element.

Fig. 6.8 *Parts cut by a robot Design of Specialised Topics, TU Graz, 2011*

2D CNC fabrication and rapid prototyping are the digital methods most frequently used for realising digitally generated conceptual, working and final scale models. Three aspects should be considered when choosing either of the two methods, the fabrication cost, the price of the material, and the cost of generating a 3D model for fabrication. Even though the costs of using these technologies have continuously dropped year after year, 2D CNC fabrication, especially laser cutting, is considerably cheaper. Choosing to laser–cut the parts of a scale model will keep the expenses relatively low, whereas the RP technology usually increases them tenfold, which is why this piece of equipment is not commonly found in architectural offices. Another advantage of 2D CNC fabrication is that it may practically be used with any material, and it also makes scale models highly tectonic. The laser technology is also applicable for a wide range of materials used in scale modelling.

Of all the previously discussed cutting technologies, the laser is the most frequently used in architectural scale modelling. This is due to the fact laser cutters are relatively small in size, user–friendly, easy to maintain and comparatively cheap. This is why in the next part we discuss the comparative advantages of laser cutting and the basic know–how needed to operate this type of CNC device in greater detail.

6.2.1   2D CNC Technology in Model Making

Laser cutting is the most cost–effective method used with sheet materials in scale modelling (Fig. 6.9). Laser cutters are easily used to cut paper, paperboard, plywood, acrylic glass and plastics (Fig. 6.10).

2D CNC fabrication may be used for operations such as engraving, cutting and assembling parts made out of sheet materials like paperboard, cardboard, plywood, acrylic glass and plastics. The parts fabricated in this way are joined together in the same way as in traditional scale modelling, but cutting the material with a machine instead of manually increases the overall precision of the modelling process.

Because all cutting is done only in the xy plane, all the parts which need to be cut are laid out or flattened in the horizontal plane for their actual dimensions to be seen. As the last preparation step, the file has to be saved in one of the 2D vector graphics formats such as .dxf (drawing exchange format, supported by all vector software). When preparing the parts for laser cutting, make sure all the drawings are "clean", which means that all vector elements may only be drawn once as single lines to prevent the laser from cutting along the same line more than once.

Fig. 6.9 *Laser cutter (left) and a detail showing the head of a laser cutter (right)*

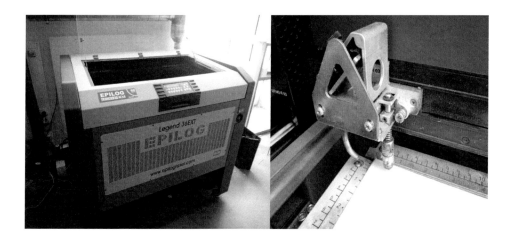

Fig. 6.10 *Model fabricated with a laser cutter. Student project, Material and Form course 2007, TU Graz*

Three basic parameters define laser cutting, the cutting speed, laser power and beam intensity. The laser beam moves along a path generated as 2D vector or raster graphics, cutting or engraving a material. The difference between the two is that to cut a material the laser beam moves at a slower pace or uses greater power. These two variables are interdependent and must be specially adjusted for use with different materials or for creating different effects. The beam diameter is 0.01 mm, which makes cutting extremely precise. The laser beam releases a great amount of energy in the form of heat, which makes it unsuitable for the processing materials like rubber or sponge, i.e., highly flammable materials or those which release poisonous gases when heated. Although paper is flammable, it may be cut with laser cutters, which are equipped with ventilation systems to help quickly remove hot air and prevent the material from catching fire.

Cutting plotters (Fig. 6.11) are 2d cutting CNC machines used for cutting only thin material such as paper or vinyl. This printer uses a knife to cut a material that is lying on the flat surface of the plotter. The plotter has a pressure control to adjust how hard the knife presses down into material, allowing full or partly cut out. The advantage compared to the laser cutter lies in being able to cut different thin flammable materials and easier handling (like a standard printer).

Fig. 6.11 Cutting plotter

6.2.2   Rapid Prototyping and Digital Fabrication

Rapid prototyping (RP) is a digital fabrication method in which thin layers of material are laid down one on top of another to generate 3D shapes. RP is also known as the additive method because new layers of material are continuously added. A virtual 3D model is prepared for additive prototyping using special software which slices it into horizontal cross–sections or parts. These cross–sections are "poured" one over another as 0,1mm–thick layers of material.

There are several RP additive manufacturing technologies, and those most commonly used in architecture are fused deposition modelling, 3D printing and stereolithography. Fused deposition modelling involves changing the physical state of a material from solid to liquid to solid to generate a model. With inkjet 3D printing, a 3D model is built from powder and a binder or adhesive.

Stereolithography, also known as photo–solidification, is based on photo–polymerisation, in which an ultraviolet laser is used to solidify a liquid material. Each of these methods has comparative strengths and weaknesses, which the modeller should be well aware of before selecting one. The geometry and intended use of the 3D model are the key factors to consider when opting for one of the RP processes mentioned above.

The preparation of 3D models for rapid prototyping is very simple, and that is the main advantage of this technology. All it takes is optimising the model relative to the scale to which it will be fabricated. The parts of the model may not be thinner than 0.51 mm; otherwise, fractures or hollow spaces may appear in the material during fabrication. Attention should also be paid to the load–carrying capacity, structural integrity and thinness or fragility of the parts to be realised.

Although preparing virtual 3D models for RP is easy, it is necessary to pay attention to the model geometry. All the surfaces of the model have to be closed and no elements may touch one another or self–intersect (there may not be double surfaces), or else the software used to prepare the design for printing (e.g., Catalyst) will report an error. 3D objects are commonly prepared for printing in the .stl format, which is supported by the majority of 3D modelling programs. Although most software applications can be used to generate a file for 3D printing, Rhinoceros is currently the best suited to the needs of rapid prototyping as it exports objects without leaving holes or gaps in the model.

Fused deposition modelling (FDM) is an additive manufacturing technology that has been used since 1991. With FDM, melted plastic is laid down in layers through a nozzle to create horizontal cross–sections. This technology uses ABS plastics, resulting in very strong models. Depending on the 3D geometry of the model, disposable support structures (usually of lesser strength) are simultaneously laid down at places where there is no base or support to deposit the principal modelling material, which are removed after the process has been finished.

The technology of FDM varies, with several materials of different physical and chemical properties used for making temporary supports. Some of them are soluble and may be removed with a diluent, while others have to be taken off physically with a pair of tweezers. Having to remove the supports physically is inconvenient when it comes to porous models, i.e., those that have holes or voids inside them, which is practically impossible and is a big disadvantage of this process. Another major drawback of FDM is that it is a very slow technology (the object shown in Fig. 6.14, which measures 5x5 cm, took four hours to fabricate). The comparative advantages of this technology are its high precision and the good structural strength and stability of the models.

Fig. 6.12, Fig. 6.13 and Fig. 6.14 show the preparation of a non–standard curtain wall element for FDM. In Fig. 6.12, we see the model ready for FD printing. Fig. 6.12a shows the entire model, and Fig. 6.12b, Fig. 6.12c and Fig. 6.12d its horizontal cross–sections, with differentiated model and support layers.

Fig. 6.13 shows a printer used for fused deposition modelling and the completed 3D model in the working space of the printer.

Fig. 6.14 shows the model on the modelling base on which it was printed, the model still joined to the support structure, and the model after removing the support.

Fig. 6.12 Using the – Catalyst software application to generate a model for digital fabrication

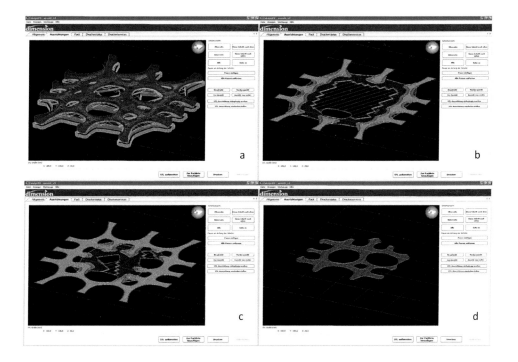

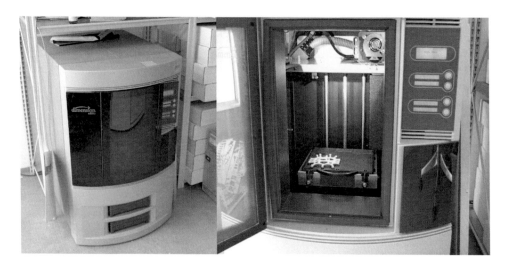

Fig. 6.13 FD printer (left) and a detail showing the modelling basket (right)

Fig. 6.14 Previously shown model with and without the support structure

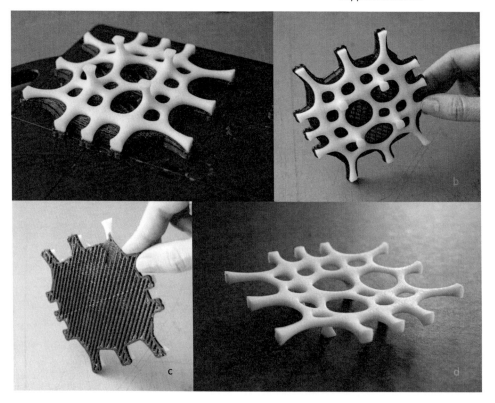

3DP modelling (also called inkjet 3D printing) is an RP technology that first appeared in the late 1990s. In this method powder solidifies after being covered with liquid acting as a binder or adhesive. After laying down powder in a horizontal layer, liquid is printed in the selected spots or parts of the cross–section. Bonded powder creates thin layers of horizontal cross–sections, which are placed one on top of the other. Liquid is printed in the way inkjet printers operate, which explains why these devices are called 3D printers. The printed model (Fig. 6.15) requires additional treatment such as removing extra powder, which is done in special rooms (spray booths) with air compressors. Finally, the model is impregnated for greater strength. This technology is simple to use, and it also allows painting the model during printing. A major drawback of 3DP is that the models manufactured in this way are brittle and easily broken.

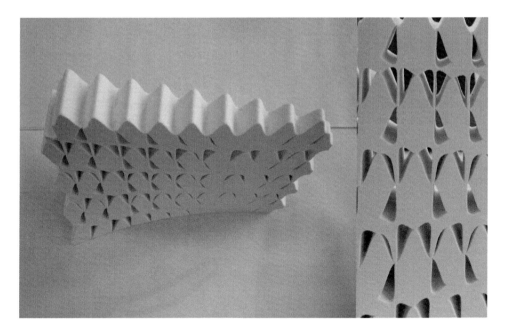

Stereolithography is the oldest RP manufacturing technology, first used as early as 1988. In stereolithography an ultraviolet laser traces the cross–section of the component pattern on the surface of liquid photopolymer, which turns solid in the process (Fig. 6.16). The model is printed by solidifying layer after layer of the polymer, whose thickness may range between 0.5 mm and 0.15 mm. This is one of the most precise and most expensive RP technologies.

Fig. 6.15 Model printed using the 3DP technology

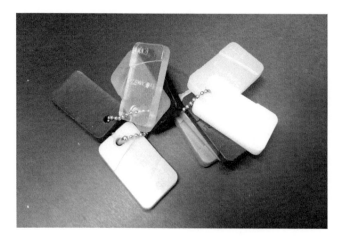

Fig. 6.16 *Different kind of material (elastic, transparent) printed with stereolithography method*

6.2.3   Reverse Engineering and Digital Fabrication

Reverse engineering is a method of generating the geometry of a building or object based on a physical 3D model with the help of a 3D scanner or micro scriber (Fig. 6.17a). The electronic pen (stylus) of the scanner is used to mark the 3D coordinates of points on the surface of the scanned object. When scanning the object, a strategy is adopted as to what points should be acquired that will allow the reconstruction of a particular surface in a CAD program. It is best to focus on the edges of the part or object and scan pre–selected points along the edge lines. 3D modelling experience advises identifying the curves generating the object under consideration and scanning the key points along those curves. CAD software shows the scanned points as points in real space.

After scanning the curvilinear geometry of the object, curved lines are interpolated through the selected points. In the case of rectilinear shapes, the end points are connected with straight lines. These lines are used to generate surfaces which are joined to form a virtual 3D model. Traditional methods may then be employed to deconstruct the generated model to produce plans and elevations.

Fig. 6.17a shows an object being scanned with a micro scriber, Fig. 6.17b shows curves selected to reconstruct the geometry of the surface(s) and Fig. 6.17c a virtual 3D model generated based on the information acquired through scanning.

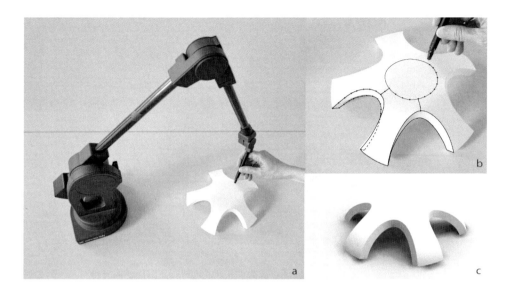

This process of generating virtual 3D models based on physical models is used by many architectural offices (e.g. Gehry and Partners) for design purposes. After analysing a model using analogue tools or building a conceptual model, the models are scanned. They are then prepared or processed for various design needs using traditional tools.

Fig. 6.17 *Scanning a model with a micro scriber*

References

[1] Autodesk AutoCAD 2013: Products. http://usa.autodesk.com/autocad/ Accessed 20 Nov 2012

[2] Kolarevic, B., (ed.): Architecture in the Digital Age: Design and Manufacturing. Taylor & Francis, Abingdon (2003)

[3] Rhinoceros 3D http://www.rhino3d.com/ Accessed 20 Nov 2012

[4] Ryder, G., Ion, B., Green, G., Harrison, D., Wood, B.: Rapid design and manufacture tools in architecture. Automation in Construction 11(3), 279– 290 (2002)

[5] Schodek D., Bechthold M., Griggs K., Kao K.M., Steinberg M.: Digital Design and Manufacturing: CAD/CAM Applications in Architecture and Design. John Wiley & Sons, New Jersey (2005)

[6] Trimble SketchUp: Products. http://www.sketchup.com/intl/en/product/index.html Accessed 20 Nov 2012

7 TUTORIALS

7 TUTORIALS

This chapter explains five different approaches to the use of digital technology in architectural form–finding research. These shapes are based on structural and geometric logic of architectural forms. The following pages give readers an overview of new scale modelling methods for folded–plate and membrane structures based on computational design, as well as the principles of modelling and digital fabrication of volumetric forms, sectioning elements and geodesic lines. Folding strategies that are crucial for the building of spatial structures, rigid and curved folding techniques are discussed in the section about folding structures, along with the geometric principles with which the process is parametricized. The segment covering membrane structures explains fundamental building logic, as well as different possibilities of software–aided form research and tensile structure construction. Innovative approaches to the application of robotic arms in the research of architectural forms are explained with examples of volumetric structure construction. The last two approaches to the application of computational design in architectural scale modelling, sectioning and geodesic lines are based on the development of linear structural elements for free–form geometric shapes. The aim of this tutorial is to provide basic guidelines for combining the computational design and digital fabrication techniques in the process of architectural scale modelling.

7.1   Folding structures

This section explains folding techniques and key strategies for the formation of spatial structures known as rigid and curved folding. It also analyses geometric particularities of folding structures made for different typological surfaces (single and double curved surfaces) and presents scale models built with different types of plate materials.The terms rigid and curved folding stand for three–dimensional structures built by following paper folding patterns. Unlike origami techniques that produce two–dimensional shapes (most commonly floral and animal shapes), folding structures produce spatial shapes with characteristic structural stability.

Rigid folding structures are built by folding planar materials while keeping all the elements planar after folding. Curved folding structures are built by folding a single curved surface so that the resulting structures are single curved elements as well (Fig. 7.1).

In architectural terminology, the term folding structures stands for structures consisting of polygonal elements. Their main characteristic is that individual polygonal elements are very small in size compared to the scale of the entire structure's bearing capacity.

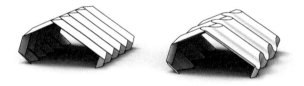

Fig. 7.1 *Rigid and curved folding structures*

Folding structures are found in many fields, such as industrial design, fashion, interior design, architecture, textile industry and jewellery. They can be made of different types of materials, such as paper, textiles, cardboard, wood or metal. Given the wide and diverse application of folding structures, literature dealing with this topic can be divided into three groups. The first group consists of literature written for designers [15],[31]. Examples found in these books are results of many years of experience. The books themselves are richly illustrated with images of different types of folding structures and their grids. Literature in the second group analyses folding structures and principles from the mathematical point of view. It is mostly scientific literature dealing with a particular topic, and it is sometimes difficult to comprehend and use in architectural modelling [32],[27],[20] [1],[4],[16],[18],[26],[5],[19]. The third group of literature discusses practical applications. It analyses the static characteristics of folding structures, taking into account the type and thickness of materials of which they are made [28],[8]. In addition to the literature, there is also FreeForm Origami software, which offers an origami simulator. This software can import pattern structures as .dxf or .obj files and simulate the folding process.

This tutorial summarises different theoretical approaches to folding with examples and focuses on geometric principles that provide the basis for the use of folding structures in architectural scale modelling.

7.1.1   Folding techniques

Folding techniques are often explored with "learning by doing" methods. The work on these structures begins with simple paper folding, playing with paper and using the simplest drawing materials. Many different forms are produced in a short time, intuitively and easily (Fig. 7.2). Folding helps to understand the physical characteristics of the material, as well as the limitations and difficulties that arise when folding different materials (paper, cardboard, polypropylene). Folding techniques also require precision and patience.

Fig. 7.2 *Intuitive modelling of different folding structures*

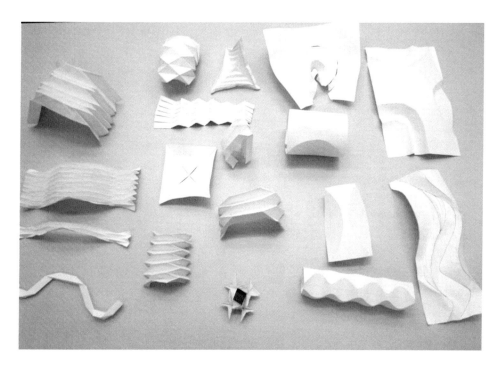

If these structures are made of paper, which allows further folding, then the simplest folding patterns can produce many different forms, as shown in Fig. 7.3 through Fig. 7.5.

Fig. 7.3 shows a cross–section of a folding structure, a phase in the folding of patterns and a completed folding structure on a single plane – planar folding. There are slots on both sides of the folding structure allowing the connection of the folds with the boundary structural elements.

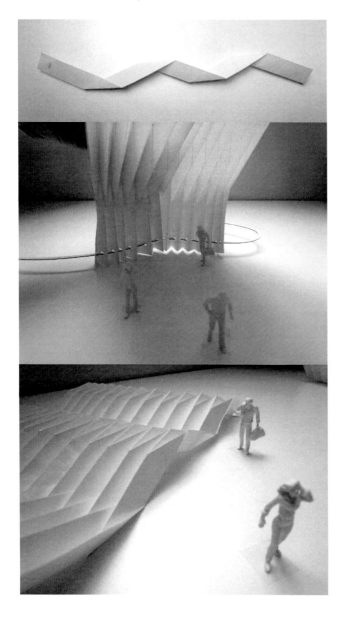

Fig. 7.3 *Basic form and a planar folding structure*

Fig. 7.4 shows a folding structure covering a quadrangular base. The figure on the bottom right shows it is possible to narrow the folds on one end. This structure is flexible because the model is made of paper, which allows for easy folding and change of angles between the individual folds. Fig. 7.5 and Fig. 7.6 show the same folding, only with a semicircle and a straight line as boundary curves. Figures on the bottom right show the possibility of opening and closing the structure if the folds are placed in a vertical position.

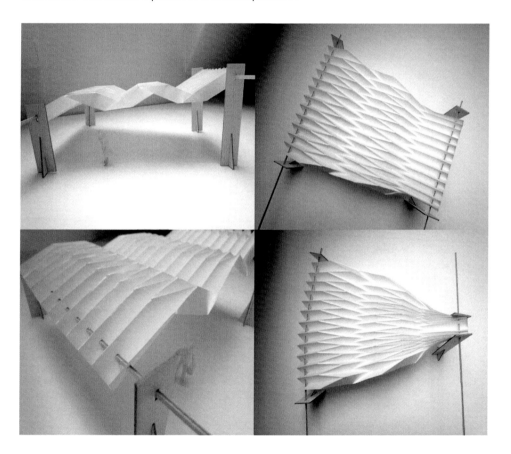

Fig. 7.7 shows the analysis of possible folding positions within a flexible system of boundary curves. Since it is made of paper, its extreme flexibility is more than obvious. This type of analysis is significant for the conceptual phase of design.

When folding structures are made of different, thicker materials, their flexibility becomes greatly limited (Fig. 7.8). It is only then that we can see the limitations and problems arising from the folding structures of considerable thick-

Fig. 7.4 Folding structure with boundary linear elements

ness. The physical characteristics of paper can lead to all kinds of wrong conclusions in the course of building a paper model. For example, paper is easy to twist out of its plane, thus changing the position of the entire three–dimensional structure.

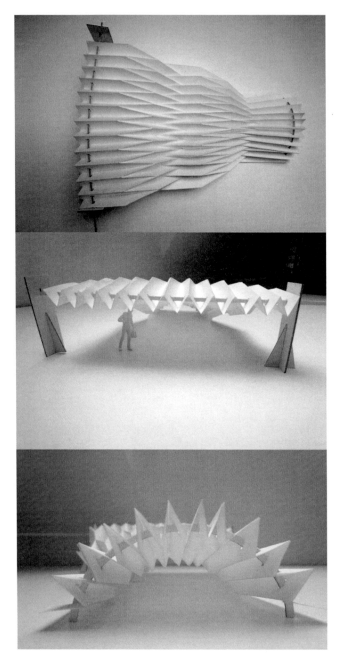

Fig. 7.5 Numerous analyses of the form with boundary curves in different positions

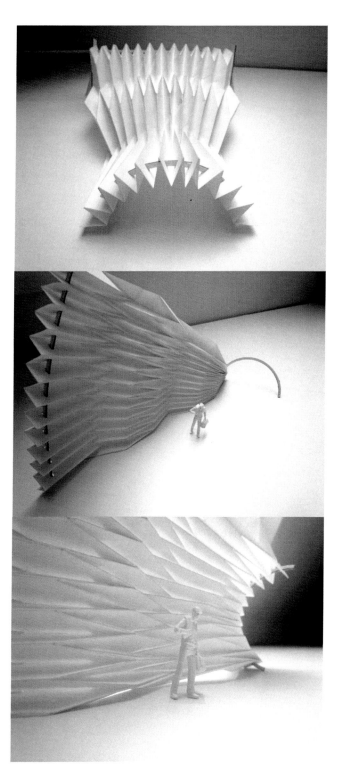

Fig. 7.6 *Numerous analyses of the form with boundary curves in different positions*

Hence, single folding structure surfaces shown in Fig. 7.3 through Fig. 7.7 are not planar elements, that is, they are not rigid structures. It is therefore necessary to use CAD tools in addition to scale models, where the entire folding element is reconstructed and its geometric characteristics controlled. This kind of control reflects on the scale model. Models are then adjusted, examined and built to reach certain conclusions that are once more tested in CAD software.

Fig. 7.7 Folding with semi-circle and a straight line as boundary lines

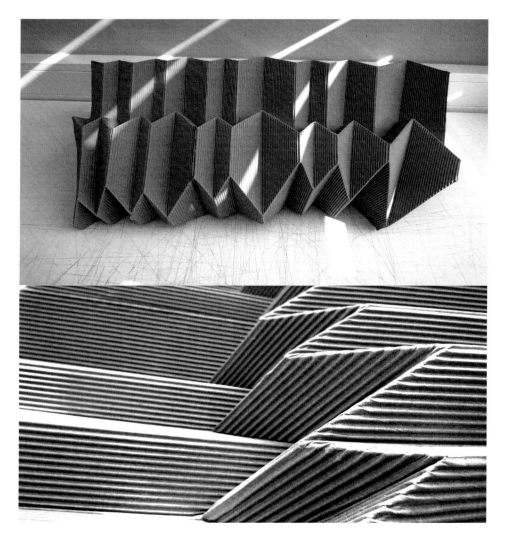

Fig. 7.8 *Scale models – folding structures*

One of the most useful methods is defining parametric models. The biggest advantage of parametric models is that, depending on the form of an object, they provide a direct connection to the folding pattern. Yet another advantage is the possibility of simulating dynamic models by opening the structure, starting from the open form position (sheet of paper) to the complete folding into a single strip.

To be able to model complex structures and generate the patterns on which paper is to be folded, one needs to understand the theory of folding. This includes knowledge of basic patterns, folding methods and understanding of spatial transformation in the folding process.

7.1.2   Basic folding patterns

Folding patterns consist of lines (rigid folding) or curves (curved folding) based on which two–dimensional materials are folded to make a three–dimensional structure. Folding alternately produces lines or curves that define mountain and valley folds.

Among the many types of folding patterns, architects are particularly interested in the Diamond Pattern, Diagonal Pattern and Miura Ori Pattern, especially their design and structural aspects. Rigid folding structures are based on these patterns. Their significance is reflected in the following:

—   They contain structural logic that gives structural stability to three–dimensional forms;
—   Basic pattern can be modified, achieving remarkable variability in the generation of three–dimensional forms;
—   Different patterns can be combined;
—   They are the basis for the development of curved folding patterns.

7.1.3   Diamond Pattern (Yoshimura Pattern)

This pattern was named after the Japanese scientist Yoshimura who observed the behaviour of thin cylinders folded under an axial compression force [19]. He found that when a cylinder is folded, its surface folds following a specific pattern resembling a diamond (Fig. 7.9).

Fig. 7.9 *A cylinder and the pattern that appears under axial pressure on the cylinder*

196

The base for this pattern is a deltoid that is folded along a diagonal. Deltoid edges are folded as a valley fold, while the diagonal is a mountain fold. A variant of this pattern can be produced if the deltoid structure is stretched following one diagonal, thus becoming a hexagonal form. In this case, instead of getting triangles we get two symmetrical trapezoids. With diamond pattern folding, all diagonals define the cylindrical polygonal line that further defines the cylindrical folding structure (Fig. 7.10).

 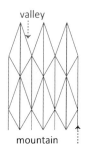

Fig. 7.10 *Diamond Pattern*

7.1.4   Diagonal Pattern

The Diagonal Pattern is very similar to the Diamond Pattern. This pattern is achieved when torsion is applied to a rotational cylinder (Fig. 7.11). The basis of this pattern is a parallelogram, folded along its diagonal. All diagonals define the valley fold, while all parallels define the mountain fold. With the Diagonal Pattern, in contrast to the Diamond Pattern, diagonal lines define helical a polygonal line, used to define helical folding structures (Fig. 7.12).

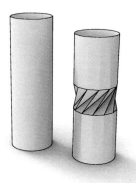

Fig. 7.11 *Diagonal Pattern as a result of cylinder torsion*

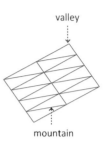

Fig. 7.12 *Diagonal Pattern*

7.1.5 Miura–Ori Pattern (Herringbone Pattern)

This pattern was named after the Japanese scientist Miura[1] who used this spatial structure system to make kinetic solar systems in space. Unlike Diagonal and Diamond patterns, whose smallest parts are triangles, the basis of the Miura–Ori Pattern is a quadrangular shape. This pattern consists of symmetric parallelograms forming a zigzag configuration in two directions (Fig. 7.13). This configuration allows for the opening of patterns in two directions. A variation of this pattern is reflected in the transformation of the parallelograms into trapezoids, which makes the fabrication of concave or convex folding structures possible.

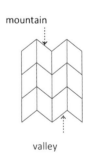

[1] *A Japanese scientist and astrophysicist, Koryo Miura created a new type of pattern in 1970 that NASA used in 1996 in the production of solar panels for the spacecraft Endeavour. The Miura–ori pattern is made up of segments – parallelograms. The entire structure using this pattern can be folded down to the size of only one segment and the only limit is the thickness of the material of which it is made. At the same time, with just one move, by pulling the opposite end, it is possible to unfold the entire structure, which is how solar panels are packed, which allows their easy unfolding in space to make a larger panel for the collection of sunbeams.*

Fig. 7.13 *Miura–Ori Pattern*

In architectural terms, it is very important to continue with the development of these three basic patterns to produce new variations of the form. This kind of research can be divided into two trends.

The first one involves the study of variations in relation to basic 2D patterns (e.g. Miura–Ori, Yoshimura, etc.) which in return generates new patterns. This method requires the understanding of folding rules and spatial relations in paper folding. The result of folding is a 3D folding structure that is actually based on one of the basic patterns, their variations, or combinations.

Fig. 7.14 shows the Ron Resch Pattern, which is a combination of a hexagonal Diamond Pattern and a Diagonal Pattern. Although this pattern is not directly applicable as a structural system due to too many degrees of freedom, it illustrates the possibilities of basic pattern development extremely well.

The second trend starts with an already known and defined 3D shape, used as the basis for the construction of the folding structure. To construct such a structure, the pattern must first be drawn. Pattern drawing requires sound knowledge of folding geometry, so the drawn two–dimensional line produces the desired three–dimensional shape after folding.

The first step towards the understanding of pattern generation is understanding of the basic folding techniques, which is the subject of the next section.

Fig. 7.14 *Ron Resch Pattern – student project, FTN – Architecture, Novi Sad*

7.1.6   Basic techniques

Fabrication of three–dimensional folding structures involves two dominant techniques: parallel folds and reverse folds. With parallel fold technique paper is folded along the lines generating alternating valley and mountain lines. Reverse folding technique changes the direction of basic folding (Fig. 7.15a). After folding around diagonal d, the mountain fold *a* turns into valley fold *b*. This way two planes become four, intersecting at point A. The position of diagonal d affects the change of folding direction.

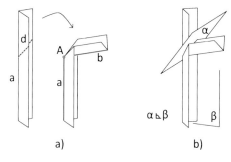

a)   b)

Fig. 7.15 a) Reverse folding b) reflection against the α–plane

Fig. 7.15b shows the reverse folding as a geometric transformation of a 3D reflection around plane α. Plane a is defined by diagonal *d*. It is perpendicular to the symmetric vertical plane β created with the parallel folding. Fig. 7.16 shows a part of such a structure with the corresponding folding pattern.

Fig. 7.16 Cylinder fold with the belonging pattern

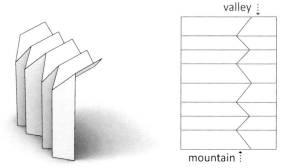

valley

mountain

If a plane is defined that is not perpendicular to the parallel folding symmetrical plane during the reverse folding process, it is possible proceed with conical folding (Fig. 7.17).

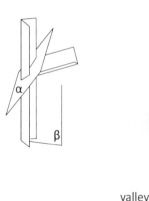

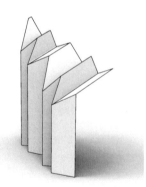

Fig. 7.17 The principle of generating conical folding, the model and the corresponding pattern

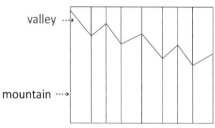

If one cylinder segment is cut like a "slice" and then rotated and combined with identical elements, the result is a "spherical" structure, shown in Fig. 7.18.

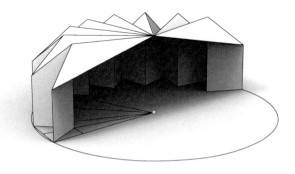

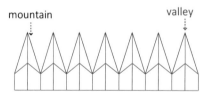

Fig. 7.18 "Spherical" folding structure with the pattern

Reverse folding is a technique that can be applied to generate curved folding. If instead of a plane we select a cylindrical surface, and then apply the reverse folding technique,
the result is a curved folding structure (Fig. 7.19). These
structures have patterns composed exclusively of curves.

Since curved folding structures result from the folding of
two–dimensional paper, the resulting surfaces can only be
single curved surfaces – cylinders, cones or tori. More complex forms of these structures can be achieved if we repeat
the primary folding several times. Fig. 7.20 and Fig. 7.21
show some of the possible complex cylindrical and conical
structures.

*Fig. 7.19 Application of re-
verse folding on an arbitrary
cylindrical surface*

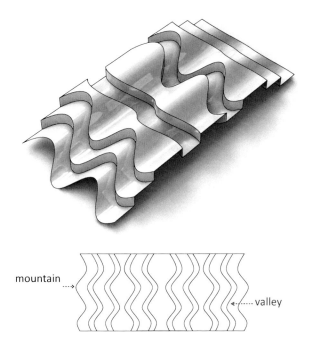

mountain

valley

*Fig. 7.20 Cylindrical struc-
ture – curved folding*

Fig. 7.21 *Conical structure –*
curved folding

If 3D models of rigid and curved folding are generated in 3D software, then it is possible to develop a folding pattern of the entire structure directly in the software (such as Rhinoceros). This is possible because each individual component is a developable surface. Naturally, it must be kept in mind that automated software solutions sometimes contain errors that need to be corrected when developing a surface. Errors can occur such as pattern overlays, and especially with complex structures, it can be difficult to orient the different parts of a pattern precisely. When patterns are first drawn, 2D drawings are generally made in CAD programs.

In the process of folding, paper is always folded along two different sides, which results in mountain and valley folds. While drawing, these lines can be marked in different colours, labelling the folding side of paper. Since folding can be complex, engraving the lines on paper helps to accurately and precisely fold the paper along the folding lines. The preparation of such patterns sometimes requires the engraving of all the mountain lines are on one side of the material and of all the valley lines on the other side.

7.1.7   Pattern generation analysis

Combining and expanding of the basic patterns requires understanding of the internal geometry of the patterns. If the geometry of folding structures is understood as a spatial transformation, then the existing patterns can be modified and combined with each other, thus providing an endless array of design variations.

In our analysis we will start with the simplest cylindrical shapes, based on a modified diamond pattern. Fig. 7.22 shows two scale models of cylindrical rigid folding structures (perspective view and top view). The cylindrical structure on the left is convex when viewed from the vertical cross–section, while the structure on the right is concave. The geometric structure of those patterns will be explained in more detail further in the text. The question architects ask when defining the structure of this form is how to fold the paper to get the rigid form shown in Fig. 7.22. The prerequisite for this structure is the possibility to make the entire fold out of a single sheet of paper, without cutting or twisting the paper out of its plane. This condition allows (if the object is made of paper) the assembly of the entire fold into a single folded strip. The final assembled position will also be the starting point for the generation of the structure's pattern.

Fig. 7.22 Convex and concave cylindrical folding structures

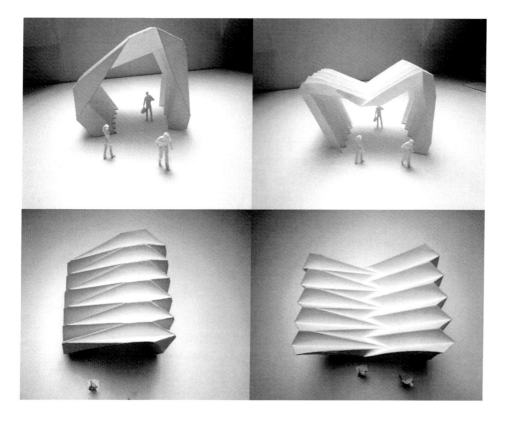

As we have seen with basic patterns, the folding structure pattern is composed of a series of polygonal or triangular elements. When these elements are folded, they assume specific positions in space so that two adjacent elements intersect along a single line, while several elements intersect at a common point. If the folding structure is composed of triangular elements, then a single point can be the intersection point of six or more adjacent polygons. If we imagine that these structures are made to the scale of 1:1, with the appropriate material thickness, then it can be very complicated to calculate and implement the intersection point of a number of different polygons. That is why we have chosen a pattern configuration consisting of trapezoids and representing a modified diamond pattern. The advantage of this pattern, compared to the triangular structure, is that up to four planes can intersect at one common intersection point.

The folding structure pattern can be calculated based on cross–sections. If a folding structure is retracted to its minimum position, then the values of all folding elements can be calculated in life size scale. After reading these values, measures can be transferred onto a sheet of paper and a structure pattern can be generated.

Fig. 7.23 shows the whole process of folding structure generation, from the original planned cross–section to the final pattern.

The convex structure example shows all the measures used to build the scale model, while the concave example shows the values in the general. The starting point for the definition of a folding structure is its cross–section. This is shaped in the form of a spline curve, shown in Fig. 7.23a. To achieve the folding structure based on the desired shape, it is necessary to approximate the curve with linear segments. To approximate this curve, we used the control polygon of the spline curve. The control points on the polygon are shown in Fig. 7.23b as 1–6, and as n1 – n7 on the concave cross–section.

For the further calculation of folds (Fig. 7.23c) it is necessary to measure the angles formed by each of the lines with the adjacent line of polygons (angle β) and measure the length of segments (a).

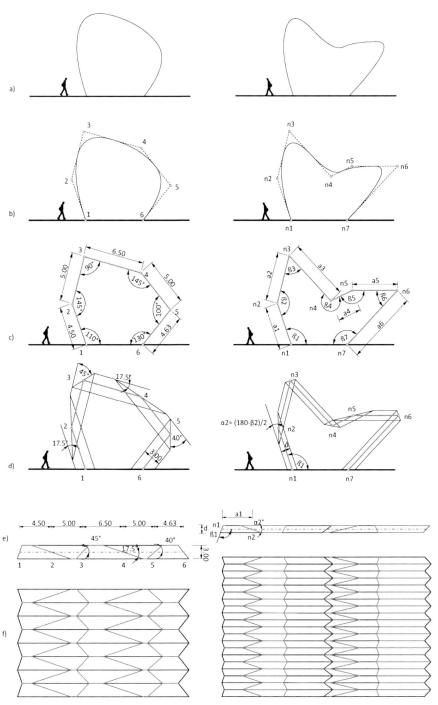

Fig. 7.23 Folding construction and calculation of the folding structure pattern

Based on these angles, it is possible to calculate the folding angle of paper at each point in the polygon:

$$\alpha= (180–\beta)/2$$

The distances between the vertices of the polygons 1–6 are distances representing the trapezoid centre lines, which define the individual structural elements. The drawn line that defines the thickness of the folds runs parallel to these edges (Fig. 7.23d). Angle α defines directions of the two un-parallel trapezoid edges, starting from the end points of the middle trapezoid lines.

Based on the values of the medium trapezoid line length (a) and angles α, it is possible to draw a grid of one segment of this fold (Fig. 7.23e). The grid is coloured in two different colours showing the two different folding directions– valley and mountain folds. Given that this is a cylindrical structure, it is necessary to mirror this segment against one of the longer edges of the folding strip to obtain the overall fold (Fig. 7.23f).

In a convex grid, all unparallel trapezoid edges are valley folds. The concave structure grid shows that in the concave part, at the vertex n4, the trapezoid edge is a mountain fold of the structure and it is precisely at this point that the structure changes direction from the convex to concave position.

A paper folding simulation can be completed after the grid has been drawn. The entire structure can be folded starting from one plane of the paper to the maximum folding position, in which the entire structure looks like a folded strip. The structure goes through various stages of folding in this process, thus enabling the generation of many different forms. Fig. 7.24 shows three arbitrary positions of the folding structure (perspective view, top view and front view).

If this folding structure is viewed as a rotation of single elements around the centre line of trapezoid elements, it is obvious that the rotation angle is somewhere in the range of 0°–90°. Fig. 7.24a shows the structure less open compared to Fig. 7.24b and Fig. 7.24c. When rotated, the fold opens more or less, thus changing the distance between the individual segments.

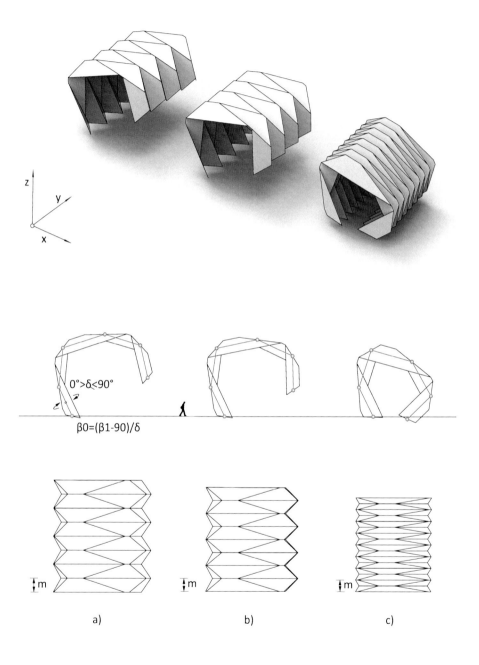

$0° > \delta < 90°$

$\beta 0 = (\beta 1 - 90)/\delta$

a)   b)   c)

Fig. 7.24 *Different opening possibilities and folding structure forms*

The *xz* plane shows different degrees of openness of these structures and the changes of angles *ß* that occur due to rotation of each individual element. The *xz* plane also shows the dependence of the first grid angle on the openness of the form. Angle $ß_0$ depends on the rotation angle and is calculated as follows:

$$ß_0=(ß_1-90)/δ$$

Based on the previously defined parameters, it can be concluded that the opening process starting from a sheet of paper to the final fold (Fig. 7.25) depends on the changes of angle *δ*. Other rotation angles are directly dependent on this angle. Such dependence allows for the parametric modelling of the entire system – from the initial form, through the grid, and finally to the animation of each individual position.

Fig. 7.25 *Fold opening*

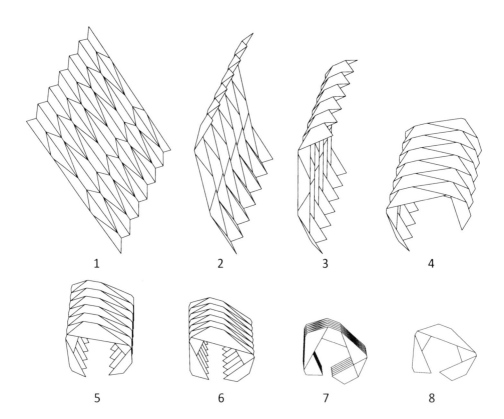

7.2 Membrane structures

Membrane structures are lightweight load–carrying structures [11],[12],[13], whose mass relative to their spanning
and bearing capacity is small. They are built from minumum
thickness materials capable of carrying the entire weight of
an object or building. As far as the mechanical properties
of these structures are concerned, a tensile load is applied
to the selected geometric shape for the purpose of form–
finding and achieving the structural integrity of the entire
system.

Modelling membrane structures requires knowledge of
their geometric and mechanical characteristics and the ability to understand the effect of the loads applied to them.

The important static property of membrane structures is
that they may be used to span large spaces while being elegant and lightweight, since only tension forces act on them.
These structures usually contain only very few compression
elements.

Spatial structures under tensile stress are designed and constructed in a way which allows them to withstand tension
without having to take any other kind of load. These structures comprise air–supported structures, cable–tensioned
structures and tensile membrane structures. They may vary
in terms of the material and type of structure used, but
they all have one geometric property in common. Namely,
they span large areas of space using a minumum of material
because of the curved shape of their surface contributing
to the overall structural integrity of the system. Achieving
the required degree of curvature may require increasing
the height of the space structure. There are two more options apart from this one and they are both concerned with
making a structural design that will ensure the loads are
transmitted in the prescribed directions. This is achieved by
tensioning the material or designing a frame so as to avoid
inducing bending stresses, i.e., optimising it to create an
ideal shape.

The geometry and physical properties of spatial structures
are best understood by building scale models, which are in-
dispensable when working with them. Tensile membranes
are also known as tents or tent–shaped structures. They are

recognisable for their pointed supports, which may take the form of tensioned cables or compression arch–like frames. Fabric is stretched between the supports to transmit the tensile stresses induced in the frame. Two types of materials are used to build membrane structures, isotropic (with identical properties in all directions) and anisotropic materials (with different properties in terms of material strength in different directions).

Doubly curved membrane structures are usually clad in two–dimensional materials; however, this is never done with a single piece of material and a cladding pattern is made which allows covering the entire structure. Individual parts of the envelope are joined together according to the pattern needed to build the desired doubly curved surface. When designing membrane structures it is very important to ensure the proper positioning of seam lines. Tensile stresses are smaller in magnitude in the area of the seam lines than in the other parts of the structure, which is why they tend to concentrate along these connections. This means the seam lines have to be positioned in the directions of the main load–carrying elements. Membrane structures are typically transluscent with prominently visible seam lines, and special attention needs to be paid to the cladding pattern and the type of connection used to join material sheets of the material.

The geometry of membrane structures is closely related to that of minimal surfaces [9]. In terms of geometry, a minimal surface is a minimal volume surface defined by its bounding curved surface(s). All membrane structures are designed aiming for the properties of minimal surfaces. Dynamic relaxation algorithms and the density method based on special discretisation and linearisation techniques are used for the structural analysis of membrane structures. Different form–finding applications have been developed to meet these special needs [17],[25],[22]. Rhino Membrane [25] is a plug–in used with Rhinoceros to generate mesh models of membrane structures. It has the capability to transform NURBS geometry into mesh geometry in a prescribed number of iterations to optimise membrane structures. Formfinder [10] is independent software used for form–finding and strain and stress analysis. It contains functions which allow the selection and analysis of structural connections and automatic cost estimation. It also has a large database of membrane structures named Projectfinder against which designs may be compared and analysed and which provides the information needed to understand and/or generate a particular structural design.

7.2.1 Design method and form–finding

The first step in the design of membrane structures does not involve making drafts such as plans, sections and elevations, which is the standard procedure of architectural design. It begins with what is known as form–finding. The process of form–finding refers to developing a prestressed equilibrium form. It consists of the following steps:

- building a physical model,
- generating a geometric model, and
- calculating static equilibrium by computer.

The building of a scale model begins by making supports. Stretch fabric is tensioned between or around the supports to observe the forces acting on the structure and modify the model accordingly. Understanding the physical properties of the model and the forces acting on the structure is essential for form–finding at this stage. Because these models are built from stretch fabric, they cannot be used to generate the pattern of a membrane structure. However, the model makes it possible to measure the degree of curvature, which may be used for geometric modelling, and the geometric model may in turn be used to model a mesh. The last stage of form–finding involves using computer software to calculate stress and strain and finalise the mesh model.

Cases are presented below illustrating the geometric modelling of membrane structures that are useful when investigating architectural forms. A membrane structure is generated as a NURBS surface on the principles of the geometry of minimal surfaces, after which the approximation method is used to generate a cutting pattern . A scale model is made to manipulate the geometric properties of the membrane structure in which deformations are observed that influence the generation of a digital model.

The properties of membrane structures are most easily examined by building a frame and using it to experiment with membrane forms. Fig. 7.26 shows this type of frame, made

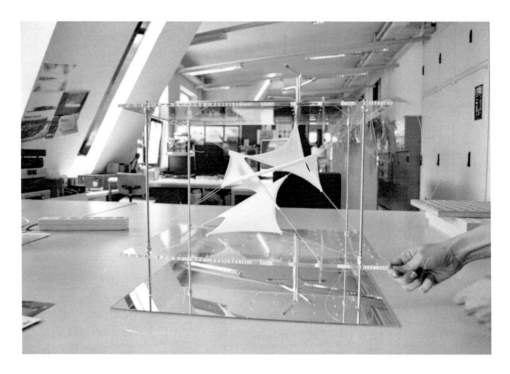

Fig. 7.26 Acrylic glass frame used for experimenting with membrane forms

of two sheets of acrylic glass placed and kept apart at an adjustable distance by height–adjustable threaded metal rods. The sheets have 2–mm–diametre holes located at grid 30x30mm. These holes serve to insert and manipulate thin cables used to stretch and tension the membranes.

The simplest tensile structure is obtained by stretching a triangle. A piece of elastic fabric shaped as a triangle is suspended in the frame and tensile stress is applied at its end points. Applying tensile forces may result in a membrane structure such as that illustrated in Fig. 7.27.

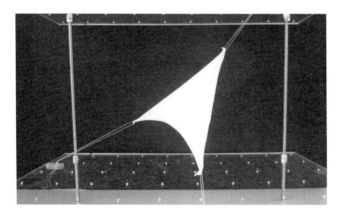

Fig. 7.27 Model of a membrane structure supported at three points

Fig. 7.28 illustrates changes to the geometry of the above structure under tension. Fig. 7.28a shows the original shape geometry, Fig. 7.28b the shape under tension, and Fig. 7.28c the construction of the change in its geometry. As the geometry of the triangle changes, the contour lines become catenary curves, which are approximated by three parabolas. The axes of the three parabolas run in the direction of the area centroid Ac.

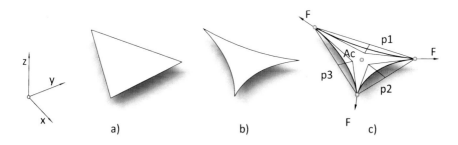

Building a sound membrane structure requires supporting it at a minimum of four points in space. This is shown in Fig. 7.29a, with the support points lettered A, B, C and D. The arrangement of the points suggests a hyperbolic parabolid of negative curvature (Fig. 7.29b). If this surface is visualised as a membrane structure, its bounding curves become parabolas (Fig. 7.29c), constructed in the same way as those illustrated in Fig. 7.27. Fig. 7.29d shows a structure modelled in Membrane 24, which is used to create mesh models of membrane structures based on the input of four support points. The model in Fig. 7.30 shows that the physical and virtual models are identical, and that when it comes to the visual aspect this approach, meets an architect's needs in the stage of conceptual design of membrane structures.

Fig. 7.28 *Basic principle of geometric change under tension*

Fig. 7.29 *Geometry of a hypar membrane structure*

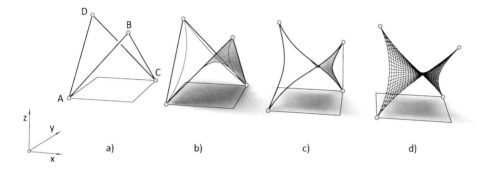

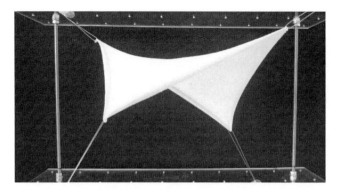

Fig. 7.30 *Scale model of a membrane structure supported at four points*

A number of membrane structures are illustrated in Fig. 7.31 and Fig. 7.32. The figures on the left (Fig. 7.31) show the basic curves needed to generate them, and the figures on the right show the membrane surfaces with the respective uv lines drawn to indicate the type of structure used. Fig. 7.32j shows complex membrane structures obtained by combining the basic types.

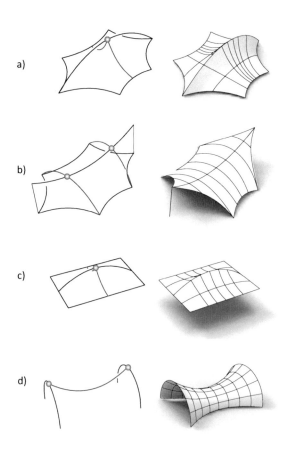

a)

b)

c)

d)

Fig. 7.31 *Various types of membrane structures*

e)

f)

g)

h)

i)

j)

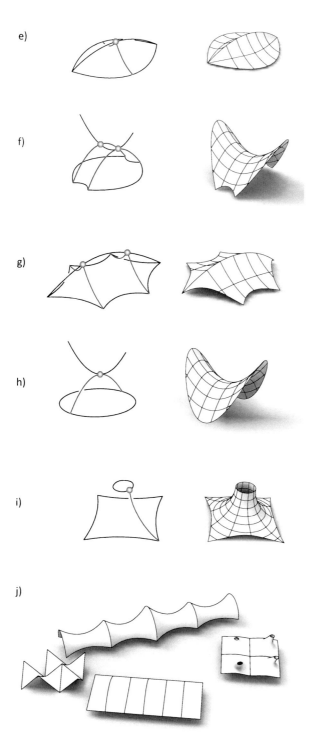

Fig. 7.32 *Various types of membrane structures*

Fig. 7.33 shows different experiments with membrane structures.

Fig. 7.33 Membrane scale models

7.3 Volumetric Structures

The introduction of rapid prototyping and the application of robotics in fabrication have made the volumetric method rather popular in scale modelling in the last few years. In this part of the tutorial we make a connection between volumetric structures and the use of robots in scale modeling to investigate the possibility of cutting volumetric materials such as XPS and EPS with hot–wire foam cutters.

One advantage of using the robot arm rather than other CNC machines to process volumetric materials is the greater number of axes and degrees of freedom of movement. The robot arm may rotate about six or more axes, making its operation more flexible in comparison with, for instance, a five–axis CNC milling machine. Another advantage is the possiblity of several robots working simultaneously, which considerably accelerates model assembly.

The robot arms are used in a range of industries, for operations that are continuously repeated an infinite number of times. The possibility of fitting the robot arm with various tools (drills, welding and vacuum tools, sensors, etc.) has resulted in the widespread application of robots in manufacturing.

The use of robots in the automotive industry is probably the best known. Car manufacturing technology, especially the assembly stage, consists of continuously repeated operations performed by robots instead of people. In such processes, the robots are programmed based on the teach method. Using a reverse engineering approach, each position of the robot is scanned and assigned an xyz value. A series of movements made by the robot travelling to the prescribed positions is the robot arm path. Special software is used to plan robot arm paths, i.e., to generate robot control codes. Robot control codes are digital statements containing sets of xyz coordinates as well as descriptions of the rotary movements of the robot arm joints needed for it to navigate from one point to the next along the planned path. Robot codes contain information concerning the robot operation speed and manner in which each specified position is reached. After a code has been generated, a simulation application is used to inspect the movement of the robot along the path to discover any potential singularities and correct the code. After the inspection simulation, the robot control code may be used in the manufacturing process. The life cycle of a manufacturing process may be several years, with up to one million repetitions, until it is superseded.

Unlike manufacturing technologies, robot arms are used for other purposes and for other applications in architectural design. In the last few years, many architecture schools have used robots for the fabrication and/or assembly of parts or objects, both for teaching and research purposes. The design of a non–standardised brick façade for a project entitled "Gantenbein Vineyard Facade", Fläsch, Switzerland by Gramazio & Kohler [7] marked the beginning of the use of robots in architectural research. A robotic production method was used to lay 20,000 bricks to form the facade of a Swiss winery building. Each brick was laid according to programmed parametres, at the desired angle and at the exact prescribed intervals, to form an architecturally unique non–standardised brick facade. The wall elements were first manufactured at the laboratories of the ETH Zürich and then transported and installed on site.

In the mean time, a number of projects have been completed in which robots were used for different operations (cutting, milling) to fabricate parts from various materials (brick, XPS, metal, wood [22], etc.), creating patterns for different uses (acoustic wall [6], spatial structures, etc.). Along with the ETH Zürich, leading schools of architecture such as Harvard and MIT have joined in robotic application research. For instance, Design Robotic Group is an ongoing project at Harvard University focusing on custom brick fabrication [2], [3]. The robotic fabrication trend [23] is undoubtedly on the rise and the only question is how its application in architectural design can be broadened.

The robot arm may be fitted with a range of tools for use in architectural design, e.g., for fabricating digitally generated parts or for non–standard assembly procedures. The fabrication of non–standard architectural building components requires planning the robot paths for each individual component due to their distinctive geometries. Therefore, it is usually necessary to generate a great number of robot navigation paths (Fig. 7.34). Each of these paths is likely to be used only once, with each new series of movements of the robot requiring planning a new path.

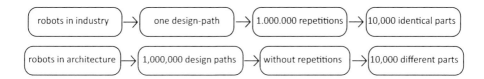

The software used for generating robot control codes is written specifically for use in manufacturing/industry. For instance, Robot Studio is one such application custom–designed by ABB for coding manufacturing processes. This and other similar applications quickly show their limitations when used for architectural design, whose needs are markedly different in comparison with how robots are used in industry.

Namely, when generating a robot control code for the needs of architectural design, the design itself is directly dependent on the capabilities of the robot arm (range of movement about axes); besides, many more control points are needed for robot path planning and all discrete robot paths have to be calculated. Unfortunately, the software developed for use in industry does not fulfill these needs. It has to be adapted by finding new ways to directly generate robot control codes based on the design. This may present a major challenge as doing it requires considerable knowledge of kinematics and of the capabilities of the robot arm. In this Tutorial, the robot control code was calculated in Grasshopper and the robot motion simulation option was used parallel to the entire modelling process.

In the next part of the Tutorial, we present two distinct cases in which the robot arm was used to fabricate volumetric models.

The first case illustrates the fabrication of 3D ornamental structures and is applicable to the design of wall elements, and the second shows how to use the robot arm to custom–fabricate concrete formwork. Considering the complexity of robotics as a discipline, this Tutorial does not discuss robot programming in great detail and only introduces the steps needed for understanding the basics of robotic fabrication.

Fig. 7.34 Differences between using robots in manufacturing industry and architectural design

7.3.1   3D Ornament

Fig. 7.35 shows an EPS model fabricated using the robot arm. The text below presents the geometric analysis of the model and the fabrication process.

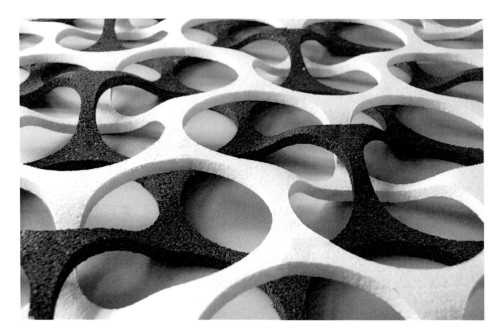

Fig. 7.36a–d shows the process of generating a 2D ornament which was used to model the 3D ornament in Fig. 7.36g. One module of the 3D ornament is generated as a cylindrical surface, with curve n as the directrix and c–direction lines as the generatrices. The contour of the module is generated as a second cylindrical surface, with straight line k as the directrix and the cylinder generatrices parallel to vertical line m (Fig. 7.36f). The geometry of this module provides the basis for generating the robot control code. The three–dimensional structure shown in Fig. 7.36h consists of two 3D ornaments. The 3D ornament in Fig. 7.36g is reflected about the xy plane and rotated 60° to generate the shape shown in Fig. 7.36h.

The thickness of the fabrication module is defined by locating a second cylindrical surface identical to and parallel with the one shown in Fig. 7.36f, with the interval between them defining the ornament depth.

Fig. 7.35 *3D ornament model consisting of 42 parts*

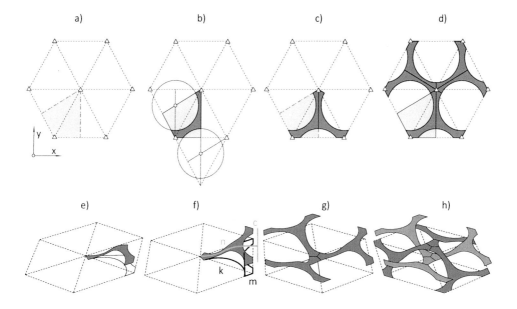

a)   b)   c)   d)

e)   f)   g)   h)

Since the geometry of this 3D ornament is defined by three cylindrical surfaces, the hot–wire cutting technique was selected for its fabrication. The robot arm was fitted with a hot wire attached to a rigid frame (the wire is heated and cuts into the material as it moves). The ornaments were cut out of EPS blocks (250x250x160mm) selected relative to the size of the robot arm (ABB IRB 140) and the hot–wire frame size.

The fabrication was done in two stages. The first stage involved cutting the modules and the second stage joining them together. Given the module geometry, the cutting had to be completed as a two–step operation. Fig. 7.37a shows the robot, the position of the EPS (Expandable Polystyrene) block and the cylindrical surface modelled after the first part of the cutting process. The second step involved rotating the block 90 degrees about its horizontal axis and cutting it along the cylindrical surface as indicated in Fig. 7.37b. The rest of the cuts were made in the z direction parallel to the last one, at distances equalling the thickness of the module.

The model was fabricated from EPS blocks in two different colours (white and gray) to highlight its undulating geometry. The analysis of the module geometry showed that seven parts could be cut out of a single block.

Fig. 7.36 *From a 2D ornament to a 3D structure*

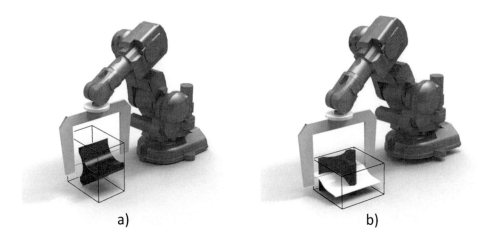

a)   b)

Cutting the parts required planning two robot motion paths and making nine different cutting patterns. The rest of the cuts, as previously said, corresponded to the last one and were made at 15–mm intervals in the z direction, which was the prescribed module thickness. Fig. 7.38 shows the cutouts, which were joined together into the structure presented in Fig. 7.35 using a hot–glue gun.

Fig. 7.37 Position of the robot arm with the tool engaged in cutting

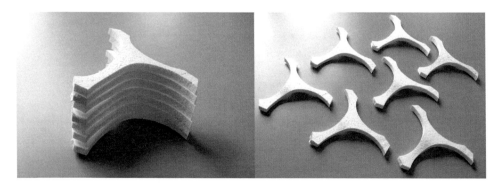

7.3.2   Concrete moulds

Fig. 7.38 Parts cut with a hot–wire foam cutter

A project was carried out on the subject of fabrication using the robot arm as part of the Design of Specialised Topics course offered in 2011 at the School of Architecture, Institute of Architecture and Media, Graz University of Technology. The assignment was to create volumetric modules from EPS for use as concrete formwork. Hot–wire cutting was the selected fabrication technique.

The focus of the project was the possibility of using standard volumetric materials like EPS for manufacturing non–standardised architectural building elements. Manufacturing non–standardised elements from standard building materials admittedly results in excessive material costs due to the use of subtractive processes in which a large amount of material is wasted during fabrication. For example, producing wooden moulds for pouring concrete to build a non–standardised doubly curved structure means every single plank has to be specially cut and processed on site by highly trained carpenters.

The project tried to solve this problem by investigating the possibility of modelling the geometry of non–standardised architectural elements that may be fabricated from standard materials using the robot arm in such a way as to ensure minimum material waste. As the fabrication was limited by the size of the robot and the standard dimensions of the material used (EPS blocks, 500x250x160mm), we chose to generate non–standardised structures consisting of modules that could be joined together after the fabrication.

The main theme of the project was generating continuous surfaces and the starting point for developing the designs was the geometric properties of wallpaper groups. Based on their 2D patterns, wallpaper groups are classified into 17 categories. The main geometric property of a 2D pattern is that it may be repeated using transformation (translation, reflection, glide reflection and rotation) to entirely cover a plane. More specifically, rotation and translation may be used to mirror two congruent figures, and reflection and glide reflection two symmetrical figures (reflection followed by translation about the reflection axis). When it comes to symmetry groups, there are only three regular tessellation patterns which may be used to entirely cover a plane. This type of tessellation is carried out with the parallelogram, equilateral triangle and regular hexagon. The unit cells of wallpaper patterns are generated by splitting these basic geometric shapes into identical secondary elements. Fig. 7.39 illustrates these basic 2D shapes, the cells generated by their splitting and the types of wallpaper groups they constitute.

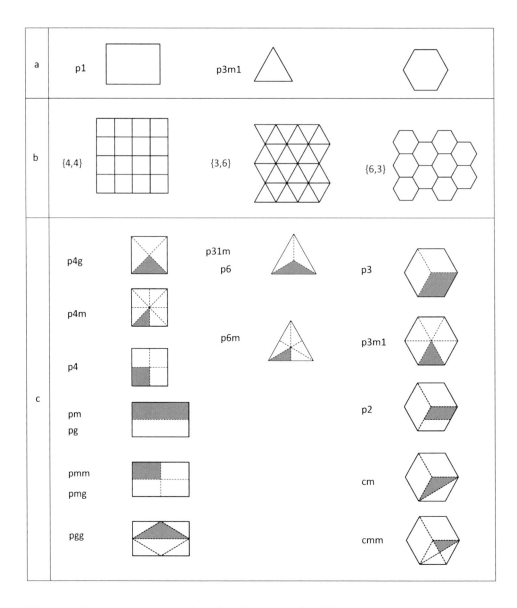

This was the approach adopted to develop and define 3D modules, i.e., volumetric objects that were fabricated from EPS blocks.

Fig. 7.40 shows an ABB IRB 140 robot arm fitted with a hot–wire foam cutter and the shapes of the blocks obtained by cutting. The wire used in the project was not simply attached to the frame (as hot–wire cutters commonly are); similar to the illustration, it may have a variety of shapes.

Fig. 7.39 a) Basic polygons used for plane tessellation, b) uniform tiling – plane tessellation by regular polygon faces, and c) the unit cells of discrete wallpaper groups

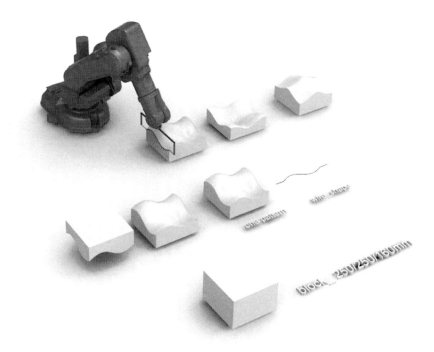

It is important to note that these volumetric models were generated only taking into account the contours of the patterns while disregarding their design and the use of colour. The students were asked to study the geometry of 2D patterns and apply their underlying principles to generating parametric 3D modular models.

The students worked in Rhinoceros to generate the parametric definitions of their models. The definitions were connected with those used for generating the robot control codes, which made it possible to harmonise the two processes. One advantage of this method is that a Rhinoceros simulation may be used to monitor the robot motion and detect any singularities in the robot path. This allowed for the possibility of simultaneously optimising the model design and robot code generation, which in turn optimised robot performance.

It is important to note that the students were asked to independently apply inverse kinematics to compute the joint trajectories along the first three axes (due to the process

Fig. 7.40 Virtual presentation of the cutting operation performed by a robot arm (ABB IRB 140) fitted with a hot wire as the cutting tool

complexity the other three were computed by the teacher) and to single–handedly operate the robot arm during the fabrication process. The students were split into pairs or groups of three for design development and fabrication. Fig. 7.41 to Fig. 7.47 show the works of the students who took part in the project, with a short description of each design.

"Wall Project"

Students: Christopher Leitner and Thomas Hörmann

The ornamental pattern is seen in the definition of the chosen surface. With the help of a single shaped wire, its different positions in space and the identification of different directrices, it is possible to create what looks like a non–standard element of very simple internal geometry.

— Translational surfaces are cut using four different patterns (but only one cutting wire – Fig. 7.41);
—   Parametric modelling allows design versatility, and makes all the generative elements changeable through the use of parameters;
—   The pattern deals with the special characteristics of the material (Fig. 7.42 upper), with the compactness and hardness of a concrete wall on the one hand and smoothness and flow on the other, which are always associated with concrete;
— The design allows multiple uses in an architectural context;
— From small–scale use, as a bar or partition (interior design), to large–scale use, as a wall element (Fig. 7.42 bottom), the form is capable of withstanding vertical loads (statics) and it can also be used as a sunshield.

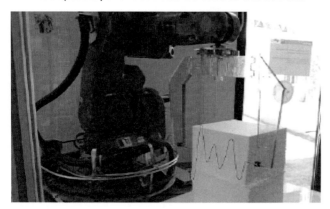

Fig. 7.41 *Robot ABB and cuting tool – shaped wire*

Fig. 7.42 *"Wall project",*
students: Christopher Leitner
and Thomas Hörmann

"Penrose Project"

Students: Georg Schrutka and Stefan Rasch

- An aperiodic pattern based on Penrose tiling (Fig. 7.43);
- Two different bricks in the form of rhombuses, one with 72° and 108° angles, and the other with 36° and 144° angles (Fig. 7.43e);
- These angles are the only invariables in the parametric model;
- The user may combine the bricks to get distinct large area patterns;
- The shape of the edges is arbitrary (Fig. 7.43a, b, c). The heights of the rhombuses at the adjoining corners have to be the same (Fig. 7.43d);
- The blocks were cut to utilise the material to the maximum. The cutting resulted in positives and negatives, which can be used for two different compositions. The attained precision can best be seen in (Fig. 7.44 bottom).

Fig. 7.43 Penrose tiling and 3D pattern

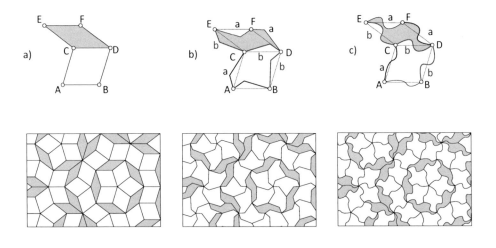

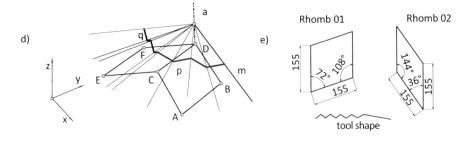

Fig. 7.44 "Penrose Project"
Fabrication and the final model

"P4 Project"

Students: Florian Maroschek and Irina Elisabeth Scheucher

- The ornament is based on the plane symmetry group p4, with one two-fold symmetry and two four-fold symmetries (Fig. 7.45a,b,c);
- Parametric modelling can be used to change the design of the mentioned symmetry groups;
- The height differences that can be seen in the patterns are due to the material thickness;
- It is possible to use only two cuts to get the four elements needed for the design, of which two positives and two negatives (Fig. 7.46). The negatives may be used as concrete formwork, and the positives as insulating wall elements;

Fig. 7.45 *P4 Ornament and 3D pattern*

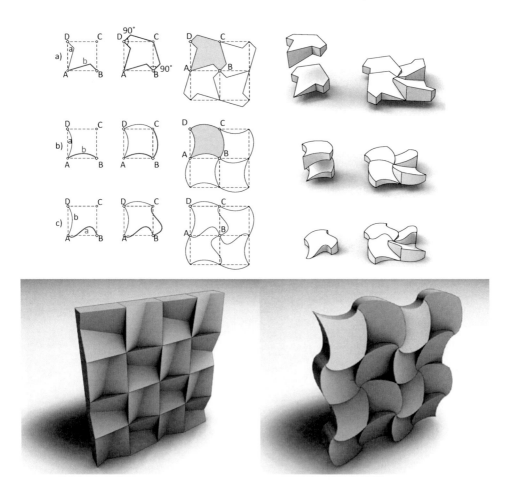

rotation + reflection (xy plane)

p4

1m²

Fig. 7.46 "P4 Project" – pattern and the final model

233

Fig. 7.47 Students projects, TU Graz

7.4 Sectioning

Sectioning is a modelling method in which two systems of cross–sections are used to generate the skeletons of three–dimensional models. The cross–sections are assembled using a system of notches. A major advantage of this method is that it may be used to represent both "orthogonal" (Fig. 7.48) and free–form geometries (Fig. 7.49) at the same level of precision and accuracy.

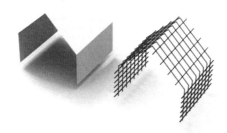

Fig. 7.48 *"Orthogonal" geometry object modelled by sectioning*

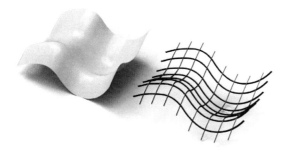

Fig. 7.49 *Free–form object modelled by sectioning*

Before using this method for scale modelling, it is essential for one to become familiar with its virtues and limitations. A major advantage of this method is that all parts of the model may be fabricated from standard two–dimensional materials. The thickness of the chosen material depends on the size of the model, its scale and the effects it is intended to achieve. When modelling orthogonal objects, the cross–sections form a framework which may be covered with planar faces to create the building envelope (Fig. 7.50a).

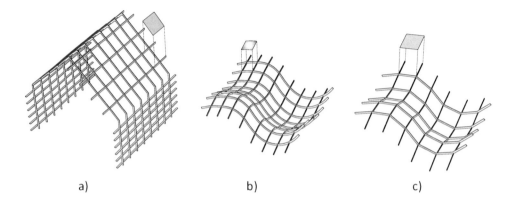

a)   b)   c)

When it comes to free–form geometries, the constituent parts are typically doubly curved, which rules out the use of planar quads (Fig. 7.50b).

If the free–form surface is a translational surface, it is possible to cover it with planar materials. One characteristic of translational surfaces is that the cross–sections remain parallel throughout the process of surface generation, which makes it possible to enclose the space between the cross–section curves with planar elements. When it comes to NURBS surfaces, the shape of the model has to be discretised. The discretisation process necessitates changing the order of curve *g* and curve *d* (Fig. 7.51a). If the degree of curvature of the b–spline curve segments is reduced to one and the resulting curved lines used to generate a surface, the resulting surface is a translational one. This surface consists of segments which are planar (Fig. 7.51b). The framework illustrated in Fig. 7.50c was generated using surface discretisation.

Fig. 7.50 *Framework covered in a) planar faces, b) curved elements, and c) a discretised surface*

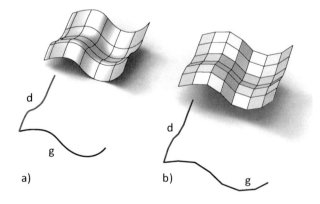

a)   b)

Fig. 7.51 *Discretisation of a doubly curved surface into smaller planar faces*

236

When sectioning is used to prepare a model for fabrication, this most often involves generating a parametric definition. Parametric definitions considerably facilitate and accelerate model realisation as they allow the changing the number of sections, their thickness relative to the thickness of the material, and the depth of notches cut into the sections. They also allow the automatic numeration of cross–sections and their preparation for laser cutting. Because parametric definitions greatly facilitate fabrication, their role in modelling sections is briefly explained further below.

When parametric modelling is done in Rhinoceros with the aim of preparing parts for fabrication, it is best to model the sections in the actual size (1:1). It is advisable to draw the model in millimetres to avoid having to round decimals. It is also best to select the size of the material that will be used for fabrication (paperboard, plywood or acrylic glass sheets or blocks) beforehand, permitting one to immediately define an optimal parametric model.

There are different ways to generate a parametric model using sectioning and different procedures may be followed. The procedure presented here serves the needs of this tutorial and it is by no means the best or the most efficient one. To illustrate sectioning, a parametric model was generated using Rhinoceros and the Grasshopper plug–in.

In the next part of this chapter we present two ways to model objects by generating sections. The first example shows how to model sections lying in two perpendicular planes. The second one presents a model consisting of a series of sectioning planes parallel to the main surface, and of another series perpendicular to it. The two examples illustrate of the ways in which sectioning may be used for free–form modelling.

7.4.1   Orthogonal sectioning

The first example illustrates the process of modelling sections to generate the free–form surface shown in Fig. 7.52a. The parametric definition of the intersecting planes requires determining the size and position of the model in space first. This is most easily done by choosing the "bounding box" command. This function specifies the maximum volume or size of the object, bounded by a cuboid whose edges are parallel to the *x, y* and *z* axes (the bounding box is marked red in Fig. 7.52a). Because the sections of the surface will be parallel to the *x* and *y* axes, the two edges parallel to these axes are extracted from the box and divided into the desired number of segments (Fig. 7.52b). The division points mark the locations of the sections of the future model. The first and last division points will not represent the actual values of the sections (they are so–called bounding values), which is why the first and last elements are removed from the list.

The generated list of division points locates the vertical planes of the model sections. The *yz*–direction planes run through the division points along the *x*–direction line, and the *xz*–direction planes through those along the *y*–direction line (Fig. 7.52c). In the next step, the surface is sectioned with these vertical planes. The generated section curves (Fig. 7.52d) are offset (Fig. 7.52e) to the required section depths and the end points of these parallel curves connect-ed to form closed curves (Fig. 7.52f). Next, these closed curves are extruded to match the width of the material that will be used to build the solid model (Fig. 7.52g). The same intersection and extrusion operations are repeated in the other direction (Fig. 7.52h). The resulting shapes are three–dimensional solid sections (Fig. 7.52i). In the next step, notches are generated for joining and fixing the sections. One series of sections is moved in the positive *z*–direction half the depths of the sections (Fig. 7.52i). This is done to vary the volumes of the sections, resulting in the series as shown in Fig. 7.52i. The same procedure is repeated for the second series of sections. The generated model is identical to the fabricated scale model (Fig. 7.52k).

A 2D drawing is extracted for fabrication purposes to de-fine the cutting paths. This is done by selecting the "explode brep" command, which extracts from the solid sections model only one surface defining each individual two–dimensional section. This command generates three lists with all the faces, edges and vertices. In this particular case, the surface defining the sections is taken from the list of the faces.

The adjoining parts are numbered at one intersection ver-tex. The last step involves laying out the sections lying in the vertical *xz* and *yz* planes and their respective marks in the *xy* plane (Fig. 7.52l).

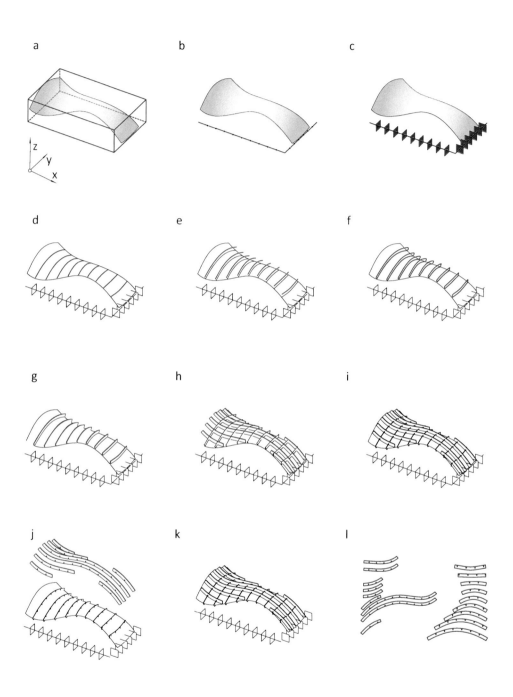

a

b

c

d

e

f

g

h

i

j

k

l

Fig. 7.52 *Procedure and steps of parametric modelling with sectioning planes parallel to the xz and yz planes*

239

Fig. 7.53 shows the parametric definition of the most important steps of the modelling procedure illustrated in Fig. 7.52. For reasons of clarity, only the locations of the *yz* sections in the *xy* plane are given. Fig. 7.54 shows the cut parts assembled into the finished model.

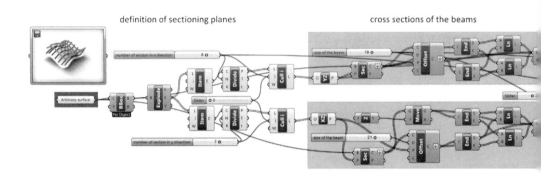

Fig. 7.54 Completed scale-model – sectioning

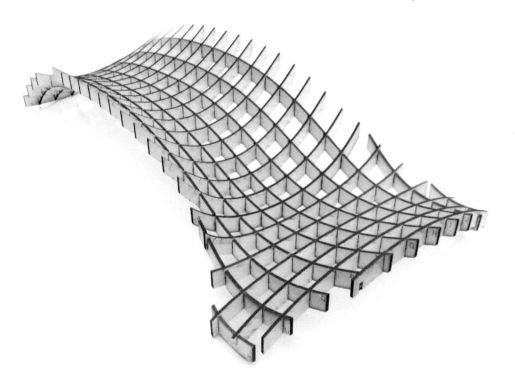

Fig. 7.53 Parametric definition of a section model in Grasshopper

solid model of the beams   connection   2d orientation onto paper space

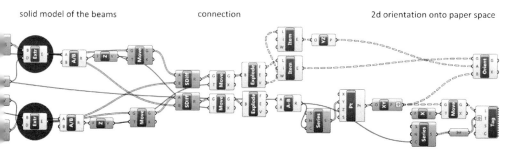

Fig. 7.55 Completed scale-model – sectionig

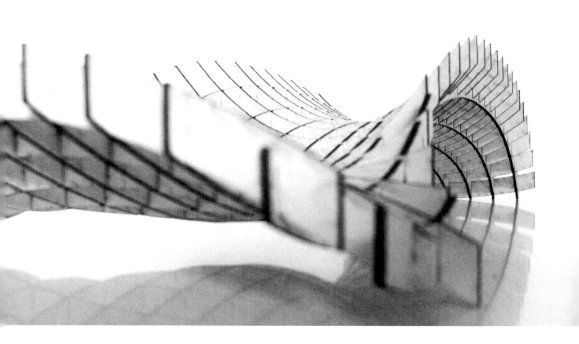

241

7.4.2 Sectioning with one–direction planes perpendicular to a surface

The next example illustrates the process of sectioning the surface shown in Fig. 7.56. This model was generated with one series of intersecting planes parallel to the x–direction and another series perpendicular to the given surface.

Fig. 7.56 *Free–form model of the cylinder topological group*

Fig. 7.57 illustrates some of the key steps in generating the sections of the model in Fig. 7.56. Fig. 7.58 shows the parametric definition.

Fig. 7.57 a shows the surface under consideration with the u and v lines drawn on it. The curves in the u–direction are open and those in the v–direction closed.

Unlike the example illustrated in Fig. 7.52, the points at which the planes intersect the surface are located by extracting one u–direction curve and one v–direction curve. A series of sectioning planes parallel to the xz–plane are located at the points dividing the u curve. The v–direction curve is intersected by a series of planes perpendicular to the surface at the division points (Fig. 7.57b). Intersecting the surface with xz–direction planes generates curves, the respective offset curves and the three–dimensional sections shown in 7.50c. If the surface is also intersected with the second series of planes, this results in it, or the corresponding parts, being cut twice by each plane. Hence, rectangles are generated instead of planes to section the surface, producing the desired section curves. The rectangle sizes are relative to the size of the object, with each rectangle cutting the surface only once (Fig. 7.57d).

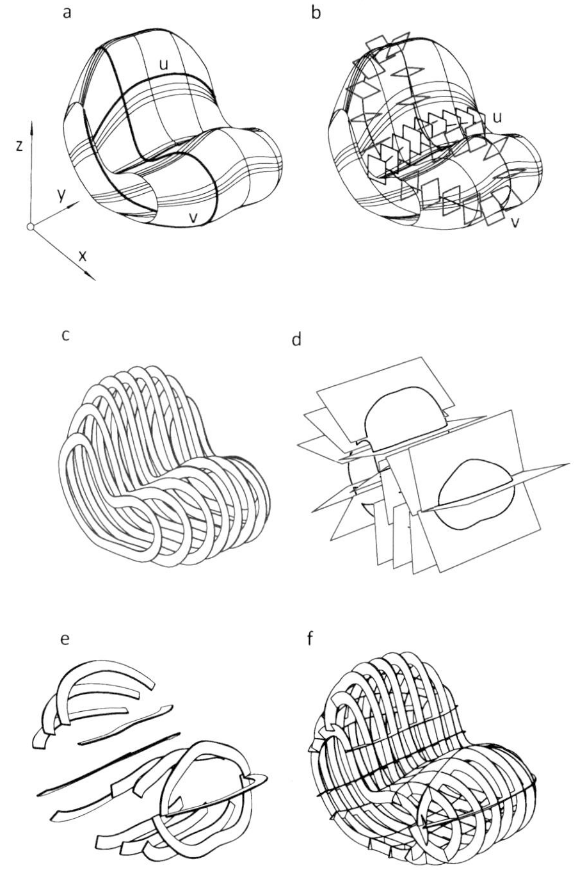

Fig. 7.57 *Some of the key steps in section modelling*

After generating the intersection lines, the cross–sections are offset and closed. In this case, the sections are extruded in the direction of the normal of the sectioning planes (Fig. 7.57e). The process of generating notches in the sections and laying the sections out on paper is identical to that presented in Fig. 7.57e.

Fig. 7.57 shows the virtual model created by sectioning and Fig. 7.59 and Fig. 7.60 the finished model fabricated using 2mm–thick paperboard.

As we said in the beginning, the parametric definitions illustrating the above examples are only possible definitions that may be used for this type of fabrication. They may be restructured to differently space out the cross–sections, make them parallel to the plane normal or to some other direction, vary their height, etc.

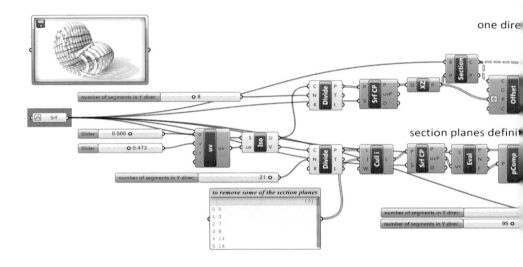

Fig. 7.59 Fabricated model

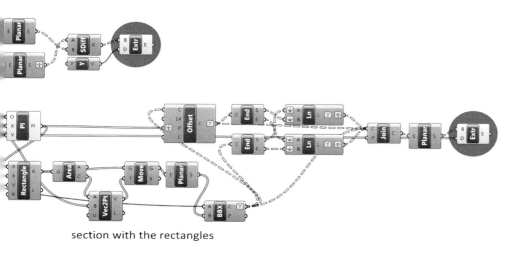

section with the rectangles

Fig. 7.60 Fabricated model

7.5   Geodesic lines

The term "geodesic lines" originated in the fields of geodesy and mapping to refer to determining the shortest path between two points on the Earth. Subsequently, the term was borrowed by mathematics and its meaning widened to reference the calculation of the shortest trajectory between two arbitrarily selected points on an arbitrarily curved surface.

The introduction of non–standard shapes in the design of architectural buildings made geodesic lines extremely appealing. Before examining their potential and the possibility to use them in architectural design, let us provide a geometric definition and outline the properties of geodesics.

A geodesic line is the shortest distance between two points lying on the same surface as the line (Fig. 7.61).

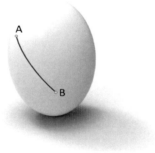

Fig. 7.61 Geodesic line as the shortest distance between point A and point B

A geodesic line on a surface may be compared to a straight line as representing the shortest distance between two points in space. The main characteristic of the geometry of geodesic lines is that they become straight lines when flattened onto a plane. This property has led to an increased application of geodesic lines and the surfaces generated around them in the architectural design of non–standard shapes. Fig. 7.62a shows a geodesic line connecting point A with point B on surface r. The line is divided by a series of arbitrarily selected points and intersected at these points by straight lines m which lie in the tangent planes to the given surface and are normal to the curve. These lines generate a surface of a certain width developable into a linear strip (Fig. 7.62b).

Fig. 7.62 Geodesic strip

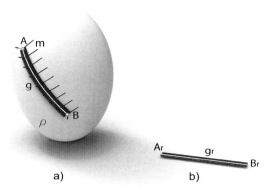

a)   b)

This means that an infinite number of strips like this may be laid out across a free–form surface, i.e., they may be used to entirely cover a doubly curved surface. When laying out a strip, it is curved in one direction, with its axis following the geodesic line and its edges running at a greater or lesser distance from the surface, depending on the thickness of the strip.

When it comes to non–standardised structural designs, the directions of the geodesic lines are often used as the directions of the load–carrying members, thus facilitating structural analysis and manufacturing. However, there is a problem to be solved in such situations, and that is the problem of laying out series of geodesic lines in one, two or three directions, while ensuring both the aesthetic appeal and structural integrity of the object or building.

Apart from building frames along geodesic lines, they may also be used to entirely cover free–form surfaces. This method is most frequently used to cover interior surfaces with boards or other linear elements. In such situations, one has to address the issue of the direction and intervals at which the strips should be laid to cover the surface with as little deformation as possible.

Fig. 7.63a shows an arbitrary surface of revolution with geodesic lines drawn in two directions, which are used to generate corresponding geodesic strips about them (Fig. 7.63b). Since this is a regular surface of revolution, it is fairly simple to generate equally spaced geodesic lines and their respective geodesic strips, creating a pattern that fully meets aesthetic design criteria.

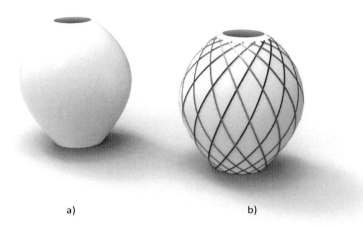

a)   b)

In this case all the lines are linear and of the same length. To fabricate a model according to this design, the end points of a strip should be fixed at a specific angle, resulting in the strips automatically generating the desired surface. Fig. 7.64a shows a non–revolution surface generated by bending the surface illustrated in Fig. 7.63.

Fig. 7.63 Surface of revolution with two series of geodesic strips

Fig. 7.64 Free–form surface with two series of quasi–geodesic strips

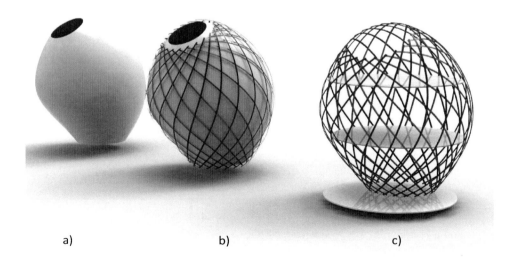

a)   b)   c)

As illustrated in Fig. 7.63b, depending on the local geometry of the given surface, it may be impossible to equally space out geodesics. If achieving an aesthetic effect is the main goal of the design, it is permitted to slightly deviate from the geodesic lines and to generate developable strips that diverge from their respective geodesic strips (Fig. 7.64b and c). These shapes differ from geodesic strips in that they may only be developed into slightly curved parts (Fig. 7.65), not into perfectly linear elements. The scale model of geodesic stripes is presents at the Fig. 7.66 and process of construction of it at the Fig. 7.67.

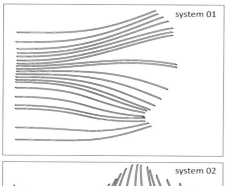

system 01

Fig. 7.65 *Quasi–geodesic strips after development*

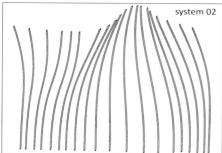

system 02

Fig. 7.66 *Scale model*

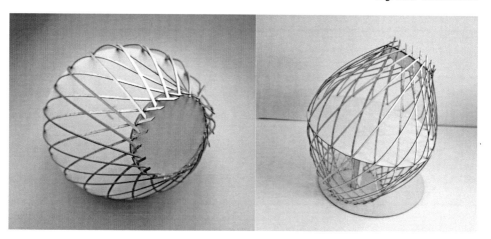

Fig. 7.67 *The scale model based on geodesic stripes in process of construction*

Publications:

[1] Balkcom,D.: Robotic origami folding. Dissertation, Carnegie Mellon University (2002)

[2] Bärtschi, R. , Knauss, M., Bonwetsch, T., Gramazio, F.,Kohler, M.: The wiggledbrickbond. In:Ceccato, C.; Hesselgren, L.; Pauly, M.; Pottmann, H.; Wallner, J. (eds.) Proceedings of Advances in Architectural Geometry 2010, pp.139–148, Springer, Wien (2010)

[3] Bechthold, M., King, J., Kane,. A., Niemasz, J., Reinhar, C.:Integrated environmental design and robotic fabrication workflow for ceramic shading systems. In: Proceedings of the 28th International Symposium on Automation and Robotics in Construction, Seoul, 29 June–2 July 2011

[4] Belcastro S.M, Hull T.C: A mathematical model for non–flat origami. In:Hull T.(ed.) Origami3, Proceedings of the 3rd International Meeting of Origami Mathematics, Science, and Education, pp. 39–51, Natick (2002)

[5] Belcastro, S.M., Hull, T.: Modelling the folding of paper into three dimensions using affine transformations. Linear Algebra and its Application(348), 273–282 (2002)

[6] Bonwetsch, T., Baertschi, R., Oesterle, S.: Adding performance criteria to digital fabrication room – acoustical information of diffuse respondent panels. In: Silicon + Skin: Biological Processes and Computation: Proceedings of the 28th Annual Conference of the Association for Computer Aided Design in Architecture (ACADIA), Minneapolis, 16–19 October 2008

[7] Bonwetsch, T., Gramazio, F., Kohler, M.,: Digitally fabricating non–standardisedbrick walls. In: Sharp D.M.(ed.)Proceedings of the 1st International Conference ManuBuild, Rotterdam (2007)

[8] Buri, H.: Origami – Folded plate structures. Dissertation, EcolePolytechniqueFederale de Lausanne (2010)

[9] Dierkes, U., Hildebrandt, S., Küster, A., Wohlrab, O: Minimal surfaces I and II. Grundlehren der mathematischen Wissenschaften, pp. 295–296, Springer, Heidelberg (1992)

[10] Form finder: http://www.formfinder.at/. Accessed 14 Jun 2012

[11] Frei, O.: Prinzip Leichtbau – Lightweight Principle. University of Stuttgart (1998)

[12] Frei, O.: Konstruktion – ein Vorschlag zur Ordnung und Beschreibung von Konstruktionen. University of Stuttgart (1992)

[13] Höller,R.: FormFindung – architektonische Grundlagen für den Entwurf von mechanisch vorgespannten Membranen und Seilnetzen. Mähringen(1999)

[14] Hunt, W.G., Ario,I.: Twist buckling and the foldable cylinder: an exercise in origami. International Journal of Non–Linear Mechanics. 40(6), 833–843 (2005)

[15] Jackson, P: Folding Techniques for Designers – From Sheet to Form. Laurence King Publisher (2011)

[16] Kawasaki, T.: On the relation between mountain–creases and valley–creases of a flat origami. In: Lang, R. (ed.) Proceedings of the First International Meeting of Origami Science and Technology, Padua (1989)

[17] Membranes 24: www.membranes24.com. Accessed 14 Jun 2012

[18] Mitani, J.: A Design method for 3d origami based on rotational sweep. Computer– aided Design and Application, 6 (1), 69–79 (2009). doi: 10.3722/cadaps.2009.69–79

[19] Miura, K.: Proposition of pseudo–cylindrical concave polyhedral shells. ISA report, University of Tokyo, No. 442 (1969)

[20] Miyazaki, S., Yasuda, T. Yokoi, S., Toriwaki J.: An origami playing simulator in the virtual space. The Journal of Visualization and Computer Animation, 7(1), 25–42 (1996)

[21] Nojima, T.: Modelling of folding patterns in flat membranes and cylinders by origami. JSME International Journal Series C,45(1), 364–370 (2002). doi: 10.1299/jsmec.45.364

[22] Oesterle, S.: Cultural performance in robotic timber construction inreForm(). In: Proceedings of ACADIA 2009, Chicago,22–25 October, 2009

[23] Payne, A.: A five–axis robotic motion controller for designers. In: Proceedings of the ACADIA 2011, Calgary, 11–16 October, 2011

[24] Pottmann, H., et al: Geodesicpatterns. In: Proceedings of the SIGGRAPH 2010, Vancouver, 7–11 August 2010

[25] Rhino membrane: http://www.ixcube.com; Accessed 22 Jun 2012

[26] Tachi, T.: Generalisation of rigid foldable quadriteralmesh origami. In: Proceedings of International Association for Shell and Spatial Structures (LASS) Symposium 2019,Universidad Politecnica de Valencia, 28 September–2 October 2009

[27] Tachi, T.: Geometric considerations for the design of rigid origami structures. In: Proceedings of International Association for Shell and Spatial Structures (LASS) Symposium 2010, Shanghai, 8–12 November

[28] Tachi, T.: Rigid–foldable thick origami. http://www.tsg.ne.jp/TT/origami/. Accessed 10 Feb 2012

[29] Tachi, T: Freeform origami. http://www.tsg.ne.jp/TT/software/#ffo Accessed 10 Feb 2012

[30] Wallner, J., et al: Tiling freeform shapes with straight panels. In: Algorithmic Methods, Advances in Architectural geometry 2010, SpringerWienNewYork, 2010, p.p. 73–86.

[31] Zeier, F: Papier – Versuche zwischen Geometrie und Spiel, Haupt Verlag (2009)

[32] Zimmer, H., Campen, M.Bommes, D.,Kobbelt, L.: Rationalization of triangle–based point–folding structures. In: Cignoni, P. Ertl,T. (eds.) Processing of Eurographics, Cagliari (2012)

INDEX

white styled models 64
wood 113
wood strips 112
working models 44

X

XPS (extruded polystyrene foam) 113

Z

Zaha Hadid 79, 142

PHOTO CREDITS

Fig. 2.8 / Page 34 - courtesy of Nikola Petković

Fig. 2.9 / Page 35 - courtesy of Christian Freissling

Fig. 2.11 / Page 36 - courtesy of Dejan Mitov

Fig. 3.1 / Page 45 - courtesy of Tamara Pavlović

Fig. 3.3 / Page 47 - courtesy of Dejan Mitov

Fig. 3.4 / Page 48 - courtesy of Dejan Mitov

Fig. 3.5 / Page 49 - courtesy of Tamara Pavlović

Fig. 3.12 / Page 54 - courtesy of Dejan Mitov

Fig. 3.14 / Page 55 - courtesy of Aleksandar Veselinović

Fig. 3.15 / Page 56 - courtesy of Dejan Mitov

Fig. 3.22 / Page 64 - courtesy of Dejan Mitov

Fig. 3.22 / Page 68 - courtesy of Marina Đurovka

Fig. 4.32 / Page 116 - courtesy of Achim Menges and Steffen Reichert

Fig. 4.33 / Page 117 - courtesy of Achim Menges and Steffen Reichert

Fig. 4.34 / Page 117 - courtesy of Achim Menges and Steffen Reichert

Fig. 4.35 / Page 118 - courtesy of Decker Yeadon LLC

Fig. 4.36 / Page 118 - courtesy of Decker Yeadon LLC

Fig. 5.30 / Page 154 - courtesy of modelArt studio

Fig. 6.1 / Page 170 - courtesy of Albert Wiltsche

Fig. 7.8 / Page 195 - courtesy of Dragana Stokić

Fig. 7.14 / Page 200 - courtesy of Dejan Mitov

Fig. 7.54 / Page 240 - courtesy of Saša Zečević

Fig. 7.55 / Page 241 - courtesy of Saša Zečević

Fig. 7.59 / Page 244 - courtesy of Maja Ilić

Fig. 7.60 / Page 245- courtesy of Maja Ilić